This Is It

This Is It

CHRIS COLBERT

Storehouse Media Group, LLC
Jacksonville, FL

This Is It

Books may be ordered through booksellers or by contacting:

Chris Colbert
Chris@ChrisColbert.com
www.ChrisColbert.com

Publishing Services:

Storehouse Media Group, LLC
Hello@StorehouseMediaGroup.com
www.StorehouseMediaGroup.com/Contact

ISBN: 978-1-943106-47-9 (hard cover)
ISBN: 978-1-943106-48-6 (ebook)

Library of Congress Control Number: 2019934380

Printed in the United States of America

dedication

For AJ, Emmett, and Annie

table of contents

Introduction i

Acknowledgments xi

Lesson 1: Evolve or Else 1

Lesson 2: The Point Really Is the Point 21

Lesson 3: You Need a Map to Realize Your Point 45

Lesson 4: Self-Love Is the Accelerant 69

Lesson 5: There Are Only Two Tribes 93

Lesson 6: Work and Life Are One 115

Lesson 7: It's All a Choice 139

To My Partners in Publishing 153

Endnotes and Bibliography 155

About the Author 159

introduction

Hi there. Welcome to *This Is It*. I wrote this book for people like you—people who believe there is something more to their lives but aren't quite sure how to achieve it. Some of you are confused, feel stuck, or feel deadened to it all, and quietly, maybe even desperately, are looking for a way forward—a path to realize your fullest possibility. I hope that is what my words provide you.

The feedback I've gotten on the book thus far has been pretty positive. But there's a caveat. Some people find it too honest, too intense, and some of the insights too intimate, too personal. I'm sorry about that, but not entirely. The truth is that in order to realize your life's possibility, you have to be willing to work hard and take risk, beginning with looking your truth, and the truth of others, in the face. There are no shortcuts, and there are no straight lines. But I guarantee you that if you do the work, you will definitely get to a better place. Right now, all you have to do is start reading.

Let's start with a bit of my own story.

I would sweat. Or drink. Or both. It would typically be a Saturday night in the suburbs. My then wife and I would be invited to a dinner party at some neighbors'. And, as always, I would be afraid. The little voice inside my head had me convinced the entire evening would be an abject failure full of awkward silences and embarrassing gaffes. So, an hour before we were due to drive to my version of hell, I'd choke down a couple of three-finger Scotches—what my mother's family used to call "dressing drinks." More like numbing aids, to calm my nerves, deaden my fears, and stem the sweat flow. All a desperately, silently frantic preparation for a genteel evening of marbled steak on the grill and gobs of red wine by the glass with people I had known for years but did not actually know at all.

And, inevitably, when I'd get to the neighbor's house, I would surreptitiously sidle toward the kitchen in order to "help," but really to avoid dreaded interactions while being knighted for my willingness to help make the dinner and clean up. Eventually, the end of the evening would arrive and my wife and I would exit, declaring what a fun night we had had while in my head I was contemplating the death march to next weekend's dinner with friends.

Good times.

So, what does this maudlin story have to do with you? Probably not that much, except perhaps the gobs of red wine and the little voice part. Or if not the vino, how about the weed, the brews, or the junk food? Whatever the substance, it doesn't really matter. What matters is whether you have someone inside your head telling you shouldn't, you couldn't, or you can't. Questioning your ability, your capacity, or your value. Or perhaps that incessant whispering has turned into an unrelenting roar of confusion. Feeling stuck? Paralyzed? Do you kinda not love your life but don't know what kind of life you love? Need a kick in the pants?

Well, here ya go.

This book is for anyone who feels stuck on the hamster wheel of life, just spinning around with no way off and no end in sight. It's for the peeps who are afraid of intimacy with others, who are confused about where to go and how to get there. It's for the increasingly desperate folks who want to drop-kick their self-doubt into the abyss and learn how to live their lives fully without fear or worry. And it's for all the seekers, the folks who are yearning to learn, but still not clear how best to proceed. My guess is that these individuals add up to a big, big number. And theirs is a big, big opportunity. As Steve Jobs said in his 2005 Stanford University commencement speech, "Your time is limited, so don't waste it living someone else's life."[1] It's true. I'm pretty sure we only get one shot, so why waste it? Better yet, why not make it the best shot ever?

Since those desperate times in the 'burbs, I have learned a ton about myself, about this thing called the human condition and about what it means and takes to live a fully realized life. The most important thing I've learned is that our capacity to engage in loving, caring, mutually beneficial relationships is the biggest determinant of a meaningful, fulfilled life. And if you don't believe me, consider *The Top Five Regrets of the Dying* by Bronnie Ware, a hospice nurse who observed that the most common regret of dying people was that they had not worked harder at intimacy and creating meaningful relationships. And if you don't believe her research, how about Will Smith, the movie star and award-winning actor who, in an interview with *USA Today* talked about the death of his father and what he had learned, sharing, "Anything that doesn't lead to a higher, more intimate relationship with yourself and others needs to be off your schedule."[2]

Yup.

The challenge, of course, is not in understanding Will's message but in realizing it, and as a result achieving a fully realized life. The journey from here to there, of innovating your Self is messy. Whether the context is work, life, or relationships with loved ones, the task of connecting intimately with someone else (including oneself) is complicated by primal instincts, faulty notions, and fundamental confusion about how to best get from here to there. And even if you have a plan, wavering motivation can throw you off.

I wrote *This Is It* to help you get to the other side, to actually break through your mental and emotional logjam to realize the fullest possibility of *your* life. Many of the ideas and observations that follow are not new. In fact, most of them have been elucidated in one form or another by minds far more brilliant than my own. The issue with many of our philosophers and self-help forefathers is not the accuracy or integrity of their insights, but the fact that their advice can be overthought, overwritten, and delivered in an inaccessible way. Which means the *%$@ doesn't stick. You read it, you contemplate it, and then you largely forget it. What's the point of all that?

My advantage and value-add to the self-help task is having over thirty years of experience as a marketer, as an entrepreneur, and most recently as the managing director at the Harvard Innovation Labs. I've built my career on the ability to understand people—what motivates them and what doesn't. My recent work at Harvard, while ostensibly focused on helping students and alumni realize the full potential of their businesses, was really about helping them learn how to connect to themselves and each other, to innovate their capacities and sensibilities in order to realize their personal and professional possibilities. The journey is fundamentally the same. And why people do and don't do what they should is at the center of the equation.

So, you can think of this book as the ultimate distillation of all the self-help platitudes that have come before, from Plato and Ghandi to Covey and Chopra, delivered in a starkly candid way that hopefully has a decent shot at causing you to break out of the morass and actually do something, and in so doing, change the trajectory and meaning of your life. *This Is It* boils down to seven simple truths, a sort of a modern-day Seven Command-ments, that you can live by in order to get more out of the life you are living. They are foundational lessons that apply across all spheres of human interaction, because whether the context is work, home, or something in between, the thing that most often stands in the way of us getting more out of life is us.

Why only seven lessons?

Because more than seven things represent too many choices for us humans, as proven by a cognitive psychologist by the name of George Miller in the '50s. He coined the term the "Magical Number Seven." Whether you buy that or not, you will agree that we are all deluged these days by information, data, advice, posts, transactions, tweets, intrusions—it's just too much. And amidst all that noise, clarity and understanding are not gained but actually lost. The self-help and business book writing industries are the poster children for too much of everything. Too much redundancy, too many parables, too many pages in most books that are drafted not to be clear but to meet some minimum page threshold. Can you remember any of it?

Too much of the same idea over and over again turns into mind-numbing reading, which in turn prompts us to give up and, worse, not remember a word. And if you can't remember whatever it is you're reading, you can't apply it, which means it can't be worth much to you. So, I'm banking that if you can remember your phone number, you have a fighting chance of remembering these lessons. God love George Miller.

This Is It was written with this construct in mind and an unwavering belief that less truly is more. Perhaps the eighth lesson! The words on the pages that follow are meant to be focused, easily understandable, and readily applicable. Follow-ing an Einstein-ism that "if you can't explain something simply, you don't understand it well enough," I have worked hard to keep it focused and crisp. No extraneous anything. The chapters are not long, but I have been told that the words are weighty—in a good way. By that I mean they are meant to be sat with and contemplated. I encourage you to take your time, read a paragraph or two, and then think about how it applies to you and what it really means. Ponder the points. Feel them. Internalize them. A little bit here and there, over time, will go a long way. I really want you to spend more time thinking about what I have to say than actually reading what I have to say.

The structure of each lesson/chapter is simple, consisting of the lesson and what it means, why it's important, what happens to us if we don't follow it, and what happens when we do. I also provide some "sub-lessons," components that hopefully make the lesson clearer and more actionable. Remember the point of all this is not to make the book interesting but to activate *your inner innovator*. The measure of success is not book sales. The measure is how many lives end up being fully lived.

To that end, there are a couple of action-enabling devices inside. The first is something called IMs. No, not Instant Messages, but Introspective Moments. These are little prompts that pop up whenever I think you should *really* think hard about what I am proposing and maybe even do a little exercise to drive the learning home. The second device, Three Things You Should Do Now, is a summary exercise at the end of every chapter. Think of this as somewhere between a call to action and a cheat sheet. This is my more overt attempt to get you to act on what I have shared quickly so that you stand a better chance of actually getting something out of this investment of your time and money. I created both devices because the last thing I want out of all this is nothing. By that I mean you and others read the book, nod politely, and then go back to your lives and jobs as if nothing happened. That would suck, for you and for me.

Why me?

I am not academically steeped in all this. I am not a shrink. But as I shared earlier, I have spent the last thirty years of my life trying to understand who I am, what was getting in my way, and by extension in the way of others in our collective quest to connect, to find our way to that place called "fulfillment" or in Albert Maslow's vernacular, "self-actualization." Along the way, I have provided counsel and consulting to hundreds if not thousands of people: employees, clients, my children, friends, and strangers. And in that counsel, I have learned that what I have to say, its clarity, its simplicity, and its meaning, seems to be helpful to people. Many have asked if I was writing a book. So, I finally decided to listen to them.

I've described my journey to others in this perhaps stark context: From childhood to age 37, I could or would not feel (remember the Scotch). From ages 37 to 45, I learned how to feel (that was a trip). And from age 45 to the present, I have become quite adept at feeling my feelings. I now understand and feel who I am; I get why I am and how I am as I stumble and skip through this thing called life. And most importantly, I am good with it all, the dark and the light. And oh, I'm not done with my journey yet.

An article I read in *Fast Company* triggered the whopping right turn in my life at age 37. The author referenced a quote by the nineteenth-century statesman Oliver Wendell Holmes, who apparently once said, "Who you are must come before what you do."

The moment I read that was jarring. I realized for the first time that I had no clue who I was and that I was hiding in my professional function. My job was a sort of suit of armor that protected me from dragons, otherwise known as people. When I was wearing the armor, I was seemingly fine. But when I took it off, I was naked and afraid. My inability to engage with others had a lot to do with that fact.

A few months later a good friend dragged me to my first-ever psychic, a rotund man with a lazy eye named Alex. Besides telling me that I was sent here from another planet (makes perfect sense to me), he kept asking me how I felt about things. And I kept answering, "I think this; I think that." Finally, he threw the deck of tarot cards at me and yelled, "I don't care what you think; I want to know what you feel!" At that moment, I realized I had no idea what he was talking about. I had no idea what I felt, because I had no idea how to feel.

That combo platter of experiences showed me in no uncertain terms that I had no clue about *me*, about what I wanted, or about how to figure it out. That ugly revelation (some would call it rock bottom) was the first step in what became a ten-year journey of gut-sucking therapy, befuddled contemplation, and heart-hurting discovery about how to find me, how to innovate me, and in doing so realize my possibility. The hard-fought journey through the dark woods resulted in me, one sunny day, standing on a sidewalk in downtown Boston at the age of 44, smiling of my own volition. For the first time in my life, I was smiling from within, without need of a joke or a joyous moment to make it happen. I was smiling because I was happy with me. I was happy with my life. It's a journey whose lessons I want to share and a journey I want to help you undertake.

But stop before you go on.

The seven *This Is It* lessons are a distillation of many other books (thank you, smart and more qualified people), my own experiences, my innovation consulting work, and my never-ending contemplation about how humans work best (or don't). One of the ancillary but essential ideas is that action is more important than words, that to learn and not act is not to learn at all. So, before you go on, consider how much you want to get to a different place and declare, ideally in writing, the level of commitment you are making to *This Is It*. Ideally set some measurable goals—in general, and specific to each individual lesson. And then try to meet them.

We all have within us the capacity to really surprise ourselves, to take off our suits of armor, and to jump over the barriers of fear and self-doubt and change the circumstance of our lives. All it really takes is walking forward, being persistent and resilient. Just trying. And in trying, I am confident you are going to realize the full possibility of your life. I believe in you. And you should too.

I thank you for coming along for this ride and being willing to consider my guidance. I hope you find my blither and spew helpful, and I hope to hear that some of it has impacted your life moving forward. You can connect with me via my monthly blog "The Blueberry" (a bite size bit of wisdom to chew on every month) at chriscolbert.com or via any of the mainstream social media channels.

I look forward to hearing from you.

Chris Colbert
Boston, 2019

acknowledgments

I could not have gotten to this place without the help of hundreds, if not thousands, of people. From Chris, the homeless guy outside the Dunkin' Donuts who provides a cheerful "Good morning!" to me every day, to the people I meet along the way who are so open and so willing to share their challenges, their truths, and their appreciation for what I have to say, everyone has helped me. And there are a certain few who were the impetus, the teachers and the cheerleaders, that really made this (and me) possible. First and foremost, Melissa Yahia, who took me under her wing and taught me how to feel. We met in college and then re-met many years later. She literally changed my life. I wish I could thank Arnold Rosoff, who passed away several years ago at the age of 93. He was an incredible man, my greatest mentor and occasional tormentor (always for good reasons), and really the only father relationship I have ever experienced. I am better, so much better, for having known and loved him. I can thank his widow Billie Rosoff, who has become my second mother, serving as a rock of wisdom and clarity, and an unconditional supporter of my own growth and evolution.

Finally, I want to thank my family. My ex-wife Mary Fahey Fields who put up with that broken man for so many years. My three kids, AJ, Emmett and Annie, who bore the weight of a father who struggled with his own truth and his capacity to love. And my wife Kate Gilbert. She has been and is an incredible partner in this journey, a cheerleader and supporter, and in a way a compelling role model for someone who didn't think they could, and then did.

To them all, I love you and thank you. To those not mentioned, the same.

evolve or else

T his is it. This is your life. And unless you believe in reincarnation, it's the only one you get. Which means, according to the latest mortality figures, you get around eighty years, plus or minus, to take full advantage of it. And sadly, terribly, most people don't even try. But my guess is because you are reading this book, you've chosen not to be like most people. You realize this is it. You've chosen to innovate. Bravo. Really.

What those other people don't realize (yet) is that you cannot achieve whatever it is you want to achieve without continuously evolving your abilities and sensibilities, until the day you leave this earth. You cannot get to a better, more fulfilling life without creating a better, more capable, more grounded you. Period. There is no entitlement at play. The American Dream, such as it is/was, accrues to those who evolve, not to those who hold on to yesterday. Or who rest on their trust fund. A large chunk of the developed world is not getting this point right now, not getting the first lesson:

Evolve or else. If you do not commit to personal growth and evolution, your ability to realize the full potential of your life is nil. Nil. Nil.

Mortality bites, and fear is ravenous.

The first order of this business is to accept that mortality is going to bite us all in the ass. Whoever said it was right: There is no escaping death (or taxes). But we are masters of delusion, operating as if there will always be another day, another opportunity to do the things we know we should do, the things we want to do. But our delusion results in delay, and delay turns into standing still. And standing still quickly converts into the feeling of being stuck, or worse, lost. We never evolve because we pretend we will live forever. And because there is something in us, a tiny, nasal-twanged voice, constantly whispering, "Don't go there, compadre!"

In his captivating book *The War of Art*, Steven Pressfield calls that annoying little voice *Resistance*. In fact, he spends half the book explaining Resistance and its incessant, multi-faceted capacity to thwart our personal evolution. His best explanation (please forgive the length) is captured here:

> "Resistance (to evolution) feeds on fear. We experience Resistance as fear. But fear of what? Fear of the consequences of following our heart. Fear of bankruptcy, fear of poverty, fear of insolvency. Fear of groveling when we try to make it our own, and of groveling when we give up and come crawling back to where we started. Fear of being selfish, of being rotten wives or disloyal husbands; fear of failing to support our families, of sacrificing their dreams for ours. Fear of betraying our race, our 'hood, our homies. Fear of throwing away the education, the training, the preparation that those we love have sacrificed so much for, that we ourselves worked our butts off for. Fear of launching into the void, of hurtling too far out there; fear of passing some point of no return, beyond which we cannot recant, cannot reverse, cannot rescind, but must live within this cocked-

up choice for the rest of our lives. Fear of madness. Fear of insanity. Fear of death."[3]

He goes on to say, in even more appropriately dramatic form:

"But they are not the real fear. Not the Master Fear, the Mother of All Fears that's so close to us that even when we verbalize it we don't believe it. Fear That We Will Succeed."[4]

Damn right, Steve.

Fear of success is the insidious monster, the fountainhead of all our reluctance to change, to evolve, to innovate, to move forward. Because success means change, right? And even if we want that change, that little voice inside us is afraid of the other changes that always come along with it. Change is the unknown, the unknown is out of our control, and being out of control means not being secure. And we really, really hate not feeling secure.

Deepak Chopra, in his book *The Seven Spiritual Laws of Success*, nails it:

"The search for security is an illusion ... actually (just) an attachment to the known. And what's the known? The known is our past. The known is nothing other than the prisoner of past conditioning. There's no evolution in that—absolutely none at all. And when there is no evolution, there is stagnation, entropy, disorder, and decay."[5]

When there is no evolution, there is decay. Deterioration. Discoloration. Yuk.

So, not evolving means decaying and other nasty things. And you cannot evolve if you are addicted to the past, the known.

You can only realize your full possibility and the potential of your future by taking the needle of the past out of your brain and learning to be fully and freely present in your heart. Sounds easy, right? But we know it's not. So, my goal in the pages that follow is to convince and motivate you to embrace the fact that your evolution, a.k.a. personal change, is not just an option but essential, and to show you some really straightforward ways to make it happen. Including telling that little voice in your head to shut the hell up.

(IM: Stop and ponder that voice right now. You can hear it, right?)

Let's dig a little deeper on why this really matters.

Darwin was right, only the fittest succeed.

So, that adage "people don't change" is antiquated crap. It should be replaced with "people must change." The world is spinning really fast, and if you don't spin in synch or faster, the centrifugal force will send you flying into outer space to float around aimlessly and eventually run out of oxygen. Nice visual.

In days of yore, not even twenty years ago, the world spun a lot more slowly. A successful life was defined by conformance and achievement of the norm: two cars in every garage, a chicken in every pot. And the inference was that just showing up got you there. The life and career path for an average American back then was a pretty simple straight line:

- Go to college
- Graduate and get a good job that more than pays off your college loans
- Get married (and don't get divorced)
- Get promoted (nice job!)

- Have kids
- Get promoted again
- Become a manager and kick back (you've paid your dues)
- Retire at 55 with a full pension

Today there is no norm, for anyone. Those guaranteed straight-line steps have been replaced by ambiguity and uncertainty. College is no guarantee of a good job. Working hard is no guarantee of a promotion. And marriage is no guarantee of staying married. And oh, the pension/retirement thing is now on you. How's your 401(k) looking?

As the standard steps to "success" have disappeared, personal and professional evolution has become a requisite for surviving, not just thriving. And it's a competitive proposition. The resources and support that may come to you could end up going to someone else. Unless you do something about it. Which is why the first questions anyone in today's hyper-competitive and -comparative world should ask themselves are as follows: "Am I endangered?" "Is the species of me vulnerable to the superiority of other members of my species? Or robots?" "Am I doing my part in adding value to the value chain?" "How can I evolve?"

If this fear pitch ain't motivating you, how about desire? How about looking at all this as an amazing, mystical, magical, impossible-to-get-your-head-around moment in human existence and your opportunity to participate in its collective evolution through your own individual evolution? Headier for sure, but it could work!

And then there's the third option, which is to be motivated to evolve by a combo platter of your stuck-ness with a nod to the opportunity, as perfectly captured in this statement often attributed to Abe Lincoln but more likely the words of a self-help author by the name of Edward Stieglitz, "It's not the years in your life that matter, it's the life in your years."[6]

Amen.

In my advisory work at the Harvard Innovation Labs and prior to that, I have had hundreds of one-on-one sessions with people young and old—starting out, mid-career, and nearing the end of their career. And many of them are in this place: feeling like their life path and current reality are just not right or where they want them to be. Some certainly getting that the new definition of success involves less about the stuff and more about the realization of Self and their unique capacities. Understanding that we have all been given a blank piece of paper, albeit with some pre-existing genomes and preconceived notions scattered about, along with some crayons and blunt scissors to create the most compelling, satisfying, and satisfied form of us, of Self. And hopefully understanding that doing so is not a formulaic set of steps but rather a messy, iterative learning journey of trial and error and, ultimately, personal growth.

I like this last one the best. Because it is motivation derived from a mix of desperation and aspiration, with a solid dash of pragmatism. You need to do this; you want to do this. You can do this. All of which increases the chances that you *will* do this.

Regardless of your motivational source code, evolution is essential. Consider this:

Your Life, the movie.

Let's just say that this life you're living—its past, present, and future, your choices, your decisions, your actions, your inactions—is all being captured via high-definition cinematography in Dolby Surround Sound. With Spielberg attempting to direct. And that at the end of your days you get to go into a movie theater with a pearly marquee that reads "Your Life" and watch the full three hours of your life story. The question is whether you stand up at the end in proud applause or walk out of the theater shaking your head. Did the lead actor or actress (you) move you? Did you marvel at their bravery and their capacity to do the right thing? Did you appreciate their thirst for learning and their willingness to embrace the unknown? Did you love how they connected with others? Particularly their loved ones? Are you fundamentally amazed at the life they lived, or horrified by the life they didn't live? And perhaps most importantly, would you recommend this movie to a friend or family member? How many Rotten Tomatoes does your life (so far) deserve?

Which brings us to the last reason evolving you matters so much.

Your Life II, the sequel.

Your life "style" and much of your storyline will be copied by others. If you have kids, they will follow in your footsteps, including standing still. If you are brave, they will be more likely to be brave. If you are curious, they will be curious. If you are open, they will probably be open. If you continue to evolve, they will be more inclined to embrace personal evolution as a requisite part of their lives.

And even if you don't have kids, you will no doubt have young people in your life who will watch you and learn from you. So, do you want to teach them the right or wrong lessons?

As I alluded to in the Introduction, the first chunk of my life story is a story of stuck-ness, not of evolution but of stasis. And my three children's early childhood was impacted by that. They began to mimic my worries, my doubts, my fears, and my fixations. I accidentally started them off down a path to the same dark, limiting place I was in. One of the best (which really means worst) examples was the day my wife and I were called in to meet with our eldest son's sixth-grade teachers. We met in a classroom, the six teachers sitting in a row, staring at us. Visualize a scene out of the Spanish Inquisition. And one by one his teachers commented on what a wonderful child AJ was, a great student and caring classmate. At the end of the lovefest I said, "While we appreciate the positive feedback about him—we love him too—I have to ask, why are we here?" And they all looked at each other sideways until one teacher finally blurted out, "We're concerned that he worries too much!" And I laughed. And then explained that he worried because I worried. Your kids will do what you do, the dark and the light, the wrong and the right. It is fundamental.

Thankfully, I was able to pull myself out of the worry muck and the negative mire, hose off the mud, and begin to work on evolving me, and in doing so, help set my children on a more meaningful, fulfilling life path. That decision and action saved me and preempted their slide into the swamp. So, if your Self isn't motivating enough to evolve you, evolve for them.

Be the director, not the stand-in.

Alongside your decision to evolve must also come your decision to actively guide your evolution, to take control of your moves (and your movie) so that you accomplish whatever it is you want to accomplish, resulting in an end-of-life standing (or perhaps lying down) ovation. Too many of us operate as if we have no say in what happens, as if the choices in our life and what's happening to us are being determined by some higher power, and we are just actors on a stage being told what to do.

In his book *Memories, Dreams, Reflections*, the early twentieth-century psychiatrist and psychoanalyst Carl Jung once wrote, "I am not what has happened to me. I am what I choose to become."[7] Choice. Everything is a choice. (See Lesson #7.) In fact, reading the rest of this book is a choice. Doing or not doing what I suggest you do is a choice. Think of it as a playbook for the big game, but you can only win the game if you execute the plays.

And if you want a quick *CliffsNotes* version of the playbook and the choices to come, here ya go:

1. Set your life's intentions.

2. Let go of all the bad stuff, beginning with fear.

3. Make your intentional choices from a position of love (of Self and others).

(Don't fret; a detailed step-by-step guide will be provided shortly.)

Making better choices and acting on them will result in (most) everything ending up where you want it to end up. But I have neglected to mention a terrible truth about all this. Even if you are mentally and emotionally prepared for this journey, parts of it will hurt.

Yes, it will hurt.

My generation grew up believing that you learned to some midpoint in your life and then rode the wave in the rest of the way. Turns out you have to keep paddling until the end. Learning later on in your life can be painful and is often exhausting. And the end is not 55; the end is the end.

The pain of personal evolution is not just about the never-ending duration of the task or one's capacity to learn, but perhaps most importantly the psychological duress associated with leaving the familiar for the unfamiliar. And it is psycholog-ical, as proven by a social psychologist named Robert Zajonc in the 1960s. He determined beyond the shadow of a doubt that people are drawn to the familiar in every aspect of life. What they like, how they decide, and the risk they are willing to take are all impacted by the comfort of the familiar versus the weight of the different.

What came to be dubbed the "mere-exposure effect," Zajonc's theory is now considered fact in the field of psychology. An article in *The Atlantic* references Zajonc's work and includes this perfect summation: "The preference for familiarity is so universal that some think it must be written into our genetic code."[8]

The familiar is, well, familiar. Comfortable, non-threatening, no surprises. We hate surprises. But in order to evolve, we must all be willing to forego much of the familiar, some of our ways of thinking (more on this a little bit later), and particularly our ways of being. Many of these ways are hardwired in us, some sourced from primal stuff, some from parents, and some from personal experience. The source mix really doesn't matter. What matters is your recognition that in order to get to the place you want to get to, you have to learn how to leave these bags on the side of the road. And saying goodbye to those bags stuffed with the familiar is hard—and painful.

I can personally attest to that.

The familiar of my existence for the first forty years of my life was really all about protection: protecting myself from the truth, from the discomfort of emotional intimacy, and from exposure to the possibility of being found out as being unworthy. I wore my business suit as that coat of armor, protecting me from having to connect with other people and with myself.

It worked for a good long time. Or I thought it worked. And then one day it didn't. I woke up and realized that there was nothing inside that suit of armor. Or more specifically, I realized that there was a scared, naked little kid in there. Afraid of the world, afraid of the truth, afraid to be.

That holy crap moment prompted a call to a friend and the beginning of a sometimes painful but ultimately cathartic ten-year journey of introspection, conversation, and contemplation of who I really was and how I wanted to be. I worked with a slate of therapists, met with more than a dozen psychics, consulted my wisest friends, and looked in the mirror often to help figure out how to let go of my incessant need to protect myself and embrace the world, the truth, and my true Self. The pain points were many, from a divorce and the loss of being with my three kids every day to the realization that my long-deceased dad had loved his Navy more than my siblings or me. Pains appeared that were associated with the past, the present, and even the future. Because the future is unknown, and that is scary and potentially painful. But I implicitly knew that the pain was necessary, that the hurt was its own form of release, and that in order to evolve I had to suffer a little and let go a lot.

(IM: What are you afraid to let go of? And more importantly, why?)

The truth stings.

As much as letting go of the familiar can be hard, so too is the task of looking in the mirror. Acknowledging the truth about our past and our present, our maybe not great choices and decisions. But you simply cannot move forward without doing this work. You have to inventory you, the good and the bad, the clear and the confused, before you have a chance to chart a path to move forward. In business terms it's sometimes called a SWOT analysis: Strengths, Weaknesses, Opportunities, and Threats. The challenges in the personal version of this exercise are how stark the reveal is, and the fact that it's not always a pleasant, something to be proud of, picture. The truth really does sting. But it also sets you free.

Failure is inevitable, and it hurts too.

The task of personal innovation is remarkably similar to the task of starting a new business. All entrepreneurs stumble and fall at one point or another. The ones who succeed are the ones who are best at getting back up after the fall, dusting themselves off, and plowing forward.

In my former role as the managing director of the Harvard Innovation Labs, I saw this on a daily basis. The startup journey has been rendered graphically by tons of "startup experts" in thousands of different ways, with lots of ups and downs being the common element. One of my favorite renditions, crafted I believe by Paul Graham, the co-founder of Y-Combinator, one of the most recognized startup accelerators, depicts two very common evolutionary and entrepreneurial scenarios: The first is referred to as "The Trough of Sorrow," the painful moment in the evolution of the business when you realize that it's all a lot harder than you imagined and that material success is not guaranteed. The second to-be-expected scenario is something called "The Pivot," the painful point when you realize that your original big idea is not that big (and maybe even bad) and you need to head in another direction.

In your personal evolution, it's highly likely that you will fall, you will fail, you will find yourself trudging through the trough of sorrow, and you will need to pivot at some point, maybe multiple times. It's also highly likely that it will hurt. But as some smart smart-ass once said, "No pain, no gain."

Curiosity creates the cat.

Assuming you're still with me, you've gotten your head around the need to evolve, and you're okay with it hurting a little, the final "to do" in getting ready for what lies ahead is to re-orient your mind to a new way of being. I call it mindfull-ness.

The misspelling is intentional. The more familiar form of mindfulness is definitely part of the equation. According to *Wherever You Go, There You Are* by mindfulness master Jon Kabat-Zimm, "Mindfulness means paying attention in a particular way: on purpose, in the present moment, and nonjudgmentally."[9] So, in order to evolve, you gotta be present, and you can't judge anything or anybody along the way. But my slightly bastardized version, mindfull-ness, includes a third facet, the importance of curiosity. The more curious you are, the more experience you consume, the more knowledge you gather, and the more full your mind, the more that mindfull-ness, coupled with the ability to be present and nonjudgmental, results in clarity.

The fact of the matter is if you don't have all the information, how in god's name can you be clear about anything?

This journey of innovating your life, the realization of your life's possibility, is first and foremost a journey of learning. It's not a simple flicking of a switch, but rather a messy, expansive, and arguably never-ending process of discovery about the truth of you, the wonders of the world, and everything in between. It's all fair and necessary game. The key is learning how to question everything without judging anything, beginning with your Self. It's learning how to explore the metaphysical and the meaning of the macro, while dissecting the micro, like why you care about how many likes your last Facebook post got.

To achieve a state of mindfull-ness you must first embrace every waking minute of every hour of every day as a classroom. And acknowledge that even your REM-level dream state can teach you a thing or two. Optimal personal learning can and should be achieved through the power of consumption: reading, observation, discussion, introspection, and retrospection. But most fundamentally through questioning. Socrates knew what he was doing.

(IM: Answer this question: Why am I reading this book, really?)

In her book *The Power of Why: Simple Questions That Lead to Success*, Amanda Lang shares:

> "The consequences of failing to do that (questioning in our personal lives) are the same as those facing businesses—even more dire, perhaps, because what's being squandered isn't just the potential for profits. It's the potential for happiness. We miss opportunities to innovate and to make positive changes in our lives when we aren't willing to question ourselves."[10]

The challenge, of course, is that questioning brings your current truth and the truth of others into, well, question. And that's where bravery enters the equation. In order to evolve, you must learn; in order to learn, you must be curious; and in order to be curious, you must be willing to question yourself; and in order to question yourself, you must be brave.

Oh, and you must be willing to walk away from everything you think you believe. Easy, peasy.

Burn your biases.

Our capacity to really understand who we are, where we are, and how we want to evolve is muddied up by our ingrained beliefs and domineering biases. Remember the importance of the familiar? Our biases are our familiar ways of viewing the world, how we determine right versus wrong, and what we like versus what we don't. Our biases have the alarming ability to make us see what is not there and not see what is. They thwart our ability to listen and serve as the archenemy of objectivity. They are the raw material that gets rendered as unfair judgment. In order to achieve mindfull-ness, you must be nonjudgmental, which means you *must* burn your biases.

The problem is that, whether we're conscious of them or not, our biases pretty much define us and they let us off the learning hook. Our nature is not to dig in, to study, and to take responsibility for knowing the facts and truths of much of anything. Our nature is not to be open to all learning in order to form our own truly individual and well-informed opinions but rather to follow our biases and declare our unfounded beliefs because, well, that's pretty much the easiest path. If you don't believe me, ask anyone you know why they voted the way they voted in the most recent presidential election. I pretty much guarantee you'll get 99 percent feelings and 1 percent facts.

As much as some of us believe that the truth will set us free, bias is so strong that it creates blinders to the facts and a remarkable capacity to reject data that clearly refutes what we believe. In fact, research shows that when people are shown data that is the opposite of what they believe, they actually believe what they believe more. That is the insidious power of bias.

The question then for you and me, and the world at large, is how to blowtorch our biases into ashes in order to learn anew and realize our possibility. I suggest that some self-reflection about a) what our particular biases are and b) where they come from may prove enlightening (and likely a wee frightening). My bet is that you'll see that our biases are one part primal, one part cultural, and two parts situational. Like the familiar, they are the combined consequence of a very distant past, our recent past, and our perceived future. And they dominate our present because we are afraid. As much as an analysis of where they came from might prove enlightening, the real task is to shut them down by opening up our minds.

You can't change the outputs without changing the inputs.

Okay, I'm going to contradict the research here. I shared that tidbit about people believing what they believe even more after being exposed to data that refutes their beliefs. Crazy. But I don't think that gives us a license to shut down the inputs, to stop trying to consume information, opinions, and perspectives that differ from our own in order to inform our own. The fact of the matter is that if you want to open your mind, to innovate your life, and to realize your most magnificent possibility, you have to open your mental floodgates to everything. The more diverse the source material, the less aligned it is with what and how you think, the greater the chance that you will be able to see the world and your Self in it differently. The more you feed your mind and soul, the greater your ability to replace your biases with new, broader points of view and the clearer your evolutionary options will become.

We're back to motivation.

Whether you're going to start hoovering up the new, torching the old, and fully embracing the task of your evolution is not a question of understanding but of motivation. After all, this is not rocket science. I know you know what I am talking about. The issue right here and now is how much do you want to change your trajectory? I believe there are only two motivators of behavior change: desperation and aspiration. Aspiration associates with "I want to do this." Desperation tends to be attached to "I need to do this." And need is a far more effective driver of action. The problem with desperation as motivation, however, is twofold: Because it conjures up fear, it can be paralyzing. So, instead of changing your behavior and taking the steps toward a different you, you just roll up into a ball and suck your thumb. You're stuck. The second issue is that most people are simply not desperate enough. Which is why I wish upon you the deepest, darkest form of desperation: rock bottom.

As proof positive of this, several months back I ended up having a heartfelt, late-night sofa conversation with someone I have known but not really known for years. For the first time in our decades-old relationship, she shared an intimate truth about her Self when she said, "I feel empty inside, and I don't know what to do about it. I'm paralyzed." I responded with empathy and understanding, and then followed with this: "I do know how you feel. That's in part why I wrote the book (*This Is It*) I sent you a couple of months ago. To help people like you and me find their way to a better place. Did you read it?" And she responded, "I tried to, but it hit too close to home." It hit too close to home, meaning it was too much truth, too much exposure for her to handle—which also means that she is simply not desperate enough to take on the demons of the truth. She has simply not hit rock bottom; she is not yet at the place where the calculation of life's upside is greater than the investment of discomfort required. And it is a calculation, as so well captured by Yoval Noah Harari in his book *21 Lessons for the 21st Century*:

> "Feelings are biochemical mechanisms that all mammals and birds use in order to quickly calculate probabilities of survival and reproduction. Feelings aren't based on intuition, inspiration or freedom. They are based on calculation. When a monkey, mouse or human sees a snake, fear arises because millions of neurons in the brain swiftly calculate the relevant data and conclude that the probability of death is high."[11]

Rock bottom is the snake, and it may be the only motivator that works.

Yup, rock bottom.

Not really, but sort of. The power of rock bottom is that it's very, very real and there is only one choice to make, one direction to take: up, or if you prefer, out. Rock bottom makes letting go really easy because you have nothing to lose. You've already lost everything. It makes risk-taking easy because you really have nothing to risk. It makes what's important really, really clear because you are no longer swimming in a murky pool of the unimportant. In a strange way, rock bottom can be the best thing that ever happens to people, enabling them to embrace the truth and motivating them to step forward boldly toward a better future, a better life.

J.K. Rowling, the prolific author of the Harry Potter series, got it exactly right in her remarks at Harvard University's 2008 Commencement:

> "I was set free, because my greatest fear had already been realized, and I was still alive, and I still had a daughter whom I adored, and I had an old typewriter and a big idea. And so rock bottom became the solid foundation on which I rebuilt my life."[12]

The other good news about rock bottom is that it comes in many forms. Certainly, I would not wish economic rock bottom like Ms. Rowling's on anyone. Or deeply psychological, depression-grade rock bottom. But there are lesser grades, part emotional, part intellectual, and 100 percent effective. I hit my own rock bottom in 1997. I was unhappy enough that I'd had enough of my Self and my inability to connect with the world around me. I simply couldn't take it anymore. And that's when I made the choice to evolve. And I moved forward.

Chris Colbert

I so want you to move forward too.

Certainly, I want you to read this book, but mostly I want you to commit to the journey of your own personal evolution, to innovate your life, and to realize your greatest possibility. I want you to see that this life you have been given is waiting for you, and that there is an amazing movie to be made by you about you. I want you not to fear the unknown and the inevitable pain that you will realize as you peel back the layers and begin to forge a new understanding of who you are and where you want to go. I want you to embrace mindfullness as the way you will be, as you open your mind and heart to all learning while letting go of the biases that confuse your truth. And while I don't wish you rock bottom, I do wish you this feeling:

> "I can't take this _____ anymore, so I am going to evolve, or else."

Three Things You Should Do Now

1. Craft a one-paragraph Rotten Tomatoes critique of the future movie *Your Life* and share it with a good friend.

2. Burn your biases. Yup, burn them. Write them down and then send them up in flames. It will feel good, I promise. Just don't do it indoors.

3. Subscribe to something new. A magazine, a TV show, a mahjong club—hell, I don't care. Just expose yourself to something that you wouldn't normally be exposed to. And contemplate how it's changing your perspective.

the point is really the point

S ince you're still reading, there's at least a 50 percent chance you know you have to evolve. That anything less is a recipe for wasting away and wasting a precious life, your only life (probably). So, now the question is evolving into what, and to where? And that is what Lesson #2 is all about.

Even if we aspire to evolve, we often feel stuck, mired in the muck of our confusion and doubt. Or absent that, we feel like we're spinning in circles, with some demonic centrifugal force creating unrelenting pressure to go around and around, leaving us with no ability to get off the not-so-merry-go-round. Or we're numb, like I was for most of my life, unable to move a mental, emotional, or physical muscle in order to improve my lot in life. Feeling paralyzed is a function of it all being too much, not being able to see our way through the mist. Feeling numb is a protective action, a psychologically induced physiological reaction to the flood of dark emotions that is overwhelming us. Regardless of the feeling, we are incapacitated and seemingly unable to push forward towards realizing our life's possibility.

Metaphor and medications aside, these kinds of feelings are real. Despite a desire for more, we often find ourselves fundamentally inert, incapable, and often pretty depressed. So, while there are plenty of "why?" questions associated with this to be plumbed later in this book, I want to start with the more imminent and actionable question of *how?* How can you begin to get unstuck, stop the spinning, regain your mobility, and start innovating your life? This question brings us to the second lesson: *The Point Really Is the Point.*

The lesson is this: *In order to get from wherever you are now to a better place, you first have to decide and define what that place is. That place is the point. I know. Stupid simple. But also, stupid effective.*

The essentiality of intentionality.

Think about it. It is brutally hard to get ahead without knowing where you want to go. Where you want to go is the definition of *ahead.* Sure, some people accidentally fall into amazing opportunities and lovely lives, and view serendipity and dumb luck as strategy. Note the term "dumb luck." Luck is not smart. And do you really want to depend on a spin of the wheel or a roll of the dice to determine your fate and future?

The challenge for many of us in our personal lives is that we know that we aren't happy or satisfied, and we know where we are right now is not working, but we don't know where we want to go. We want change, but we have no clear vision of what that actually means. So, we sink and spin, and spin some more. The only way to get off your ass and start moving forward is to pick a point, a destination. Intention is everything. And when I say intention, I mean both defining a measurable outcome *and* declaring the motivation to get there. The point.

No intention, no *specific* desired outcomes, likely no action. Apply Lesson #2 to the common task of dieting and weight loss via a hypothetical conversation between two friends:

Alison: I really want to lose weight.

Gerry: Why? You look great (fibbing). How much weight?

Alison: I don't know. I haven't decided.

Gerry: What are you going to do to lose weight?

Alison: I don't know because I don't know how much weight I want to lose.

The absence of a point in Alison's dream of losing weight negates the opportunity for a plan. You simply cannot create a road map for a journey that has no declared destination. The point, the destination, is everything. Stephen Covey, in his 25-million-copy bestseller *7 Habits of Highly Effective People,* declares via his Habit #2 that we must "Begin with the End in Mind."[13] Exactly— the point really is the point! And so, assuming that every reader of his book seeks to become more effective, the question readers should end and begin with is "What is the definition of effective?" That's the point of reading that book, right?

And if you don't define the point of reading *this* book in some measurable way, you cannot know whether you are making progress toward it. Simply put, there is this:

That which is not measured cannot be improved upon.

Think about it for a second. How the hell can you improve on something if a) you haven't defined what improved means (the point) and b) you aren't measuring your progress toward that point?

It's silly. And yet it happens all the time.

Back to the Alison and Gerry conversation, three months later:

Alison: I think I've lost some weight.

Gerry: How much weight? You look great (fibbing again).

Alison: I don't know; I'm not weighing myself. I don't want to get hung up on numbers.

Gerry: Are you on a plan?

Alison: Not really. I've just kinda been trying to eat better and walk more.

Gerry: Is it working?

Alison: I don't know. I think my face looks thinner. But I'm having a hard time making good choices and staying on track.

The absence of a point is a surrogate signal of a lack of commitment. But worse, it actually kills your motivation. How can you stay on track if you don't have a track plotted out? Imagine trying to win a game with no goals, no end zones, and no scoring. There's literally no potential to win; "winning" means nothing in this context. Playing such a game fundamentally conflicts with human behavior and our needs to achieve and to win. There's a good reason why most people enjoy sports and other competitions, even on a friendly level. Charles Darwin was and still is right. We are hardwired and hard-coded to beat the other guy, to fight for our survival. We love winners.

And yet in both our personal and professional lives, we undertake all sorts of endeavors with no points in mind. What's going on here? On the one hand, we want definitions of success and clear measures of winning, and on the other hand, we seem to avoid putting stakes in the ground on what constitutes reaching our points. Why the dissonance?

Most simply, the absence of a point, a measure of success, quite brilliantly lets us off the hook. No point, no accountability—to Self, to partner, to boss, to anybody. I also believe that we avoid creating points on personal undertakings that either carry the risk of failure (also known as shame) or are so complex that we struggle to distill them down to a simple, single point. As much as we want to win, we hate to fail more. And as smart as we think we are, some of this stuff is really messy and hard to sort out. So, what do we do? We avoid setting our intentions; we don't establish a point. We just sink, spin, and sit. Also known as lather, rinse, repeat! It is a deadly cycle that can only be broken by defining our points: the point for our future, the points for our actions, and even the point for things like parenting.

So, what's the point of parenting?

According to the last U.S. Census of the 250 million adults in America, about 45 percent are parents. And in taking on that role, they all take on a huge responsibility to develop their children for their adult future. I'd suggest that in this case there is a collective understanding of the general point of parenting: something like happy, contented, confident kids. *But* rarely do parents really put a stake in the ground on what they're after for their children; rarely do they define the point, document the point, review the point, and most importantly, assess their parenting actions against their kids' movement toward the point.

Why not? Again, because we don't want to fail. If we don't define the point in tangible, measurable terms, then no one can accuse us of being terrible parents. Perfect! And if we don't define the point, we don't have to work so hard at being effective parents. In fact, we can leave most of what happens to our kids to chance. If we love them a lot and teach them a little, it will all work out just right, right?

Not quite. In her *New York Times* piece titled "The Antidepressant Generation," Dr. Doris Iarovici, a psychiatrist and researcher at Duke University, shared a stunning stat: From 1994 to 2006, the percentage of students treated at college counseling centers who were using antidepressants nearly tripled, from 9 percent to over 23 percent.[14] Depression is now the number one issue on college campuses, trumping drugs and alcohol. Jesus.

The summary point about the point of parenting: If you want your kid to be happy, make it a point. And then make a plan to help make that happen. See Lesson #3. And then hold your Self accountable to that plan. See Lesson #7.

Now let's get to the general topic of your point.

Missing the point.

I know what you're thinking. How do I find and define my point when I'm not exactly sure what I'm after? First, stop thinking about this as material gain. Stuff is not a point. It can be a derivative of other points, meaning you can get the goods you want once you get to how you want to be and why.

Did you catch that?

I said *how* you want to be, not *where*. So, the funny thing about defining your point is that it's not really a place. Bill George, the author of the book *True North*, describes it this way:

> "It is your orienting point—your fixed point in a spinning world—that helps you stay on track. Your True North (your point) is based on what is most

important to you, your most cherished values, your passions and motivations, the sources of satisfaction in your life."[15]

So, it's not a place. It's a way; it's a why.

Why is far more important than *where* or *what*. *Why* is the connector, the meaning maker, the purpose part of your personal equation. Good points often include a Why. It's so important that it deserves to be capitalized.

Some examples of good points, good Whys, are "I want to make my living off my creativity so that I can realize my gift," or "I want to be surrounded with caring friends so that I can feel the wonder of love," or how about "I want to live an honest, authentic life so I can be free." A big-ass house so you can impress your friends is not a good point. And the reason why is because a big house won't care for you, it won't make you feel whole, it won't give you freedom, and it certainly won't be top of mind as you exit this world.

My point, my Why, is to help a lot of people. In part because I don't want you to waste a big chunk of your life like I did. And in part because I am grateful for all that I have learned and simply want to share it with as many people as possible. And perhaps finally, because a psychic once told me that I was sent here to help people. So, I'm just doing what I was told. I'm Mork. You're Mindy.

Helping thousands, maybe even millions, is my Big, Hairy, Audacious Point or BHAP, a slight twist on the idea of a BHAG or "Big Hairy Audacious Goal"[16] concocted by Jim Collins and Jerry Porras in their 1994 book *Built to Last: Successful Habits of Visionary Companies*. My BHAP is my Why, the motivating context for everything I do and why I do it. My Why doesn't make me a saint; it just makes me me.

While no one knows exactly who said this, it's spot on: "The two most important days in your life are the day you are born and the day you find out why."[17]

Exactly.

A slightly more contemporary bloke by the name of Simon Sinek calls all this the "Golden Circle,"[18] a framework to help us all realize that the Why of anything, and I mean anything—a person, a product, a cause—carries 90 percent of the power and the value. The what and the how are the way to the Why. More specifically, the how of you is the means of achieving your point. In my case it's through sharing, advising, teaching, and motivating. The what is through my consulting, my speaking, and hopefully through this book.

What's a good point?

People love exact, simple definitions for complex, nuanced things, even though they tend not to really exist. So, I am going to play along. I've tried to convey that a good point, an effective and motivating point, is a point that captures the way you want to be and the Why of you. If that's not quite clear enough, how about this:

> Your Point = Passion (Why of you) + Unique Capacities (What of you) x Desired Nature of Existence (How you want to be)

Your point can be partially determined by first adding your Passion to your Unique Capacities. That combination of your Why and What will begin to reveal the truth about where you want to go, where you want to evolve. *But* the exponential factor, the force multiplier, is the Desired Nature of the Existence you seek, the How you want to be. It's a multiplier versus an additive because the tone of our lives has such a huge impact on how we feel about our lives. Our environment, the people in it, the energy

28

we experience, the love we realize (or don't), is the greatest contributor to both our ability to see our point and to achieve it. The Nature of our Existence informs everything.

(IM: Take your time with this equation. Think about it for five minutes. Yup, five minutes, before you keep reading.)

Now, let's drill down into each variable in the formula a bit more.

The concept of *Passion* is simple. It's what you love, what you care about, what floats your boat. This is the Why stuff. It does *not* have to be complicated. Mine is helping people. Period. You can be passionate about learning, about creating, about solving problems, about exploring, about pretty much anything. There is passion in each of us; there is passion in you. You just need to bring it to the surface. Read on for some help on how to do that.

Unique Capacities is more complicated. I call this your One Simple Thing or OST. What's your standout ability/sensibility that defines you? This is the What stuff. What's the simple label that your friends put on you? (And they do put a label on you, my friend, they do). Do this exercise today: Ask one or more of your family or friends what one word or short phrase they most associate with you. I guarantee they will blurt something out in seconds. In my old life, before I unstuck myself, my One Simple Thing was "Intense." Ninety percent of the people I knew slapped me with that not-so-warm-and-fuzzy label. Ouch. Now that I'm on the other side, they've given me a new OST. And it's "Inspired Possibility." My friends, co-workers, and clients tell me that I motivate them to see and realize new possibilities. And that seems exactly right.

Desired Nature of Existence is the How you want to be. This is the murkiest of the three for sure, but it really is the most important. This is a declaration of the kind of life you want to live as measured by the interactions within it. Think about the tone and pace of your day-to-day existence, about how you want it to be, about the kinds of people and influences you want to surround yourself with. The Desired Nature of our Existence is the lubricant for us realizing our Passion and unlocking the full power of our Unique Capacities. Kinda gross, I know. But true.

How to find your point.

First things first: Drop the desperation at the door. It has served its purpose to get you going, but now that you're into actually doing the work, you need to move into a more aspirational mode. Sustained desperation becomes negative energy, and negative energy begets negative crap. Positive energy gets you the good stuff. And that is scientific fact. In the late '90s, psychologist and researcher Barbara Frederickson determined something she called the Broaden and Build theory. It's a pretty-much-proven framework that shows how positive emotions open us up to opportunities while negative emotions, like fear, doubt, and anger, result in narrower responses. Positive feelings, positive energy, and positive attitudes beget positive things. Period. Feelings like joy, appreciation, contentment, love, and self-love all tend to render good stuff coming back at you. And contrary to perception, more often than not, positive feelings are a choice. See Lesson #7.

Makes sense, right?

So, the only way to find your point is to approach the task in positive peace mode. Positive as in excited, believing, hopeful, and joyful. Peace as in Zen, chill, cool with the journey, and gently girded for whatever you dig up. This is going to be fun.

Okay, not really. But it will be enlightening and clarifying, and in that there should be a smile or two. Like much of the advice that follows in this book, achieving positive peace and your point does not happen with the flicking of a switch. There ain't no switch. In other words, you can't go from being Eeyore to being Christopher Robin overnight. What you can do is work at it.

Now I want you to think about what it is you want relative to how you want to feel, what gives you joy, and why it makes your heart feel alive. Yup, your heart. I know it sounds a little soft and gushy, but it turns out your heart actually has more happiness capacity than your brain. So, every now and then it's healthy and not woo-woo to listen to it. And if you don't believe me, how about this little ditty from *Seven Spiritual Laws of Success* by the master of self-help, Deepak Chopra: "At times it may not even seem rational, but the heart has a computing ability that is far more accurate and far more precise than anything within the limits of rational thought."[19] What he said.

When people talk about what they want in material terms, for example, a new house, a new job, a new nose, they are really talking about the feelings they want to have that they think are associated with those things. They want the new house because they subconsciously think it will make them happier, and in some cases, even solve their marital issues. A realtor I once worked with shared an observation that for certain kinds of couples, the buying of a new home was often a last-gasp attempt to save the marriage, and it never works. Divorce proceedings ensue right after the first mortgage payment. Houses don't fix interpersonal issues, new noses don't always create confidence, and new jobs don't always rekindle passions. Sure, they can help, but in truth we can realize the feelings we want without those things. In fact, we'd be better off if we did.

I could now reel off a series of adages that are all getting at the same idea. How's "Money can't buy you happiness" or

"It's about the journey, not the destination" for starters? What those ageless clichés are trying to get at is a happy life is not defined by what's in it, but who is in it and how you are in it. And how deeply you are connected with the who. Sure, money makes things easier. But easier does not necessarily translate into happier. In fact, money can confuse you into thinking that you've got it made when in fact you haven't got *you*. And you can't buy you; you have to *make* you. And the way to do that is not to trawl for a new house but instead to innovate you.

Now hear this:

Get out of the myopic tunnel you are in and open all of yourself up to experience. The only way to figure out where you want to be is to experience as much of what exists out there as you can and how you co-exist with it. I spoke at a conference recently, and a young woman asked me how she could find her passion. My response was twofold: You must first experience as much as you can, and then you must feel how it all feels while you experience it. Experience people, experience places, experience things, experience knowledge, experience risk, experience discomfort—experience everything.

The ostrich with its head in the sand metaphor comes to mind. You cannot see if your head is stuck in the sand. The challenge is that digging your head out of the sand does not require a shovel, it requires guts. Yup. The reason why people don't expose themselves to new experiences is more often a function of fear than it is desire. As I shared in Chapter One, we fear failure, we fear rejection, we fear loss, we fear god—we fear everything. Fear is the great inhibitor in our lives. That's the bad news. The good news is that fear is a choice. Everything is a choice (see Lesson #7). But fear is the big one.

Garrett McNamara, the *Guinness Book of World Records* record holder for riding the biggest wave ever (100 feet), probably understands the fear factor better than anyone. In his recent autobiography *Hound of the Sea* he shares "... fear is a choice, something we manufacture in our minds. When we think about the past or the future, we become afraid. We're afraid because we remember when something bad happened before, and we're scared it's going to happen again. If we're in the moment and enjoying the moment and making the best of the moment, there is no fear."[20]

Garrett's suggestion that fear correlates with our thoughts of past or present is spot on. And primal. The fact is we are not that far removed from our caveman ancestors. We still fear the wooly mammoth, the saber-toothed tiger, and the bolts of lightning thrown by the angry gods. We fear not being able to protect ourselves, we fear exposure to danger, we fear the potential of suffering and not being able to provide, we fear being cast out of the tribe. Hell, we fear failure in virtually every form.

(IM: Ponder the last time you felt fear and write down what made you feel that way.)

We don't take steps toward the unknown because the unknown petrifies us. We don't take steps toward people we don't know at cocktail parties because they petrify us. We are primal creatures, and strangers represent a threat, like the saber-toothed tiger did.

The unknown and the new scare the hell out of us. And that's why setting goals does too.

We avoid setting goals for ourselves *not* because defining them is that hard but because we fear not reaching them. Reread Lesson #1.

Think about management guru Peter Drucker's SMART goal-setting framework: S = Specific, M = Measurable, A = Assignable (who owns it), R = Realistic, and T = Timetable for achievement. Pretty simple, right? But not really. Because when we put pen to paper, when we get specific, we get real, and when we commit, we are on the hook. And the prospect of that is alarming. So, we don't do it.

And oddly enough, we also don't like to make goals because we fear achieving them. What, you say? It's true, it's true. Some percentage of us want what we want but don't want the change that comes with it. There's that fear of the unknown again. Getting to your point, to your goals, means getting to a different place. And deep inside the recesses of our minds, difference connotes risk. That point of success carries new dynamics of how you are going to exist. Old friends might not understand, partners might be jealous, people might want what you have, and you might end up being lonely. There's a gaggle of saber-toothed tigers wrapped up in the fear of setting and reaching our points, our goals. But hey, if big wave surfer Garrett McNamara can eschew fear when three trillion tons of Mother Nature's force are crashing down around him, I think you can decide to not choose fear too. Not every time, but more and more often.

So, suck it up in order to mix it up.

I want you to take the next few weeks at work, at home, anywhere, to suck it up (the fear, that is) in order to mix it up. Try new things, say hello to new people, go to new places, explore. Eleanor Roosevelt (remember her?) once said something like "Everyone should take a little risk each day." Great advice. A little risk goes a long way in helping you get your head out of your . . . um, out of the sand. The risk thing can really be *any* risk.

Here are some toe in the water, get your head out of the sand risks:

- Ask your boss for a raise, or even for some constructive feedback.

- Order the strangest thing on the menu.

- Wear that outfit that you've never worn—you know the one I mean.

- Introduce yourself to the guy or gal at the gym who you see every day.

- Volunteer to work at a food pantry.

- Thank a friend for being a friend.

- Do all of the above.

Think of your risk capacity as a muscle. It's in you; it's just a little atrophied. Time to exercise it. And while you do, observe yourself. I think of this as the act of removing myself from myself. You are now a higher being, watching your human Self take risk and engage with foreign stuff. Congratulations! It's also your chance to be a morally responsible voyeur! Look closely and look often.

Watch your Self.

Watch for the moments that make you smile, that make you feel good, as well as those that make you feel not so good. What is going on in them? What parts of your Unique Capacities are at play? How is your entire physiology responding to the task or person? What is happening? And why? Again, why is key. As much as you might feel rudderless and without control of what's happening before you, it's actually not true. Each and every day you are making subconscious choices that align with what makes you feel either good or bad. Focus on understanding the choices that make you feel good, and start making more of them, damn it, assuming they're healthy choices, of course! The Why is that connection between the choice and the motivation, the good feeling. I choose to have dinner parties. They make me feel happy, and I feel happy because I get to be creative and care for people at the same time. Oh, and I love delicious food. The cleanup, not so much.

Write down what you observe. Separate your observations into three buckets: Passion stuff, Unique Capacity stuff, and Desired Nature of Existence stuff. As an example, I did this exercise myself, observing my life experiences this past week:

Passion

Met with ten Harvard students on their startup ideas and helped craft their business plans while giving them hope that they can realize them. Loved seeing them get clearer, and their appreciation for my time and insights didn't hurt.

Had two dinner parties in a row, Saturday and Sunday nights. Made an entire Indian meal for both nights, lots of cumin! Really fun to cook all day, if a little exhausting. Combination of creative energy and logistical prowess. Guests loved it, and we have plenty of leftovers. Yum.

Unique Capacities

Met with some of my direct reports regarding their performance and professional growth. Focused on helping them stretch, define their goals and near-term actions. Really meaningful conversations. Felt good to give them direction and a little motivation.

Spoke at a conference about Personal Branding and marketing oneself. People came up to me afterward, excited about the possibility of it all and asking to meet with me. Some even asked if I was writing a book, sharing that my observations were really helpful. Hurrah!

Desired Nature of Existence

Kate and I attended a couple of arts events. Loved being with artists and supporters of the arts. Open-minded, aesthetic creatures, not a dull mind in the bunch. All much smarter than me. Really fun and motivating for me.

Met with an MIT PhD startup founder. Talked about genomics. Way out of my league but learned a ton about double helixes and felt grateful to have such brilliance in my life.

Don't overthink this exercise. Just focus on capturing the actions, decisions, and interactions that made you feel good, that "fed" you, and that felt like your true and most admirable Self being you.

Keep it going with a little help from your friends.

Sometimes doing this work can start feeling a little insular, perhaps a little too much like belly-button gazing. So, ask your friends what they think the best parts of you are, and why. Another fear-full situation! It will take courage to do this. Some of your pals might not have much to say, which you're going to construe as you not having "best parts." But don't go there. What you should construe is that they simply don't know you that well. Some might have too much to say, and it might start feeling creepy. Bring it to a close, gently. Write down what you hear on a piece of paper, or better yet, in a journal.

A graduate student advisee of mine at Harvard did this exercise and interviewed sixty friends. That's a lot. Five to ten should suffice. But interestingly, the feedback he got was remarkably consistent. And when we worked through the long list together, the descriptors reduced down to a handful, and ultimately a couple, of really clear reveals. His Passion is to solve complex, global problems, and his Unique Capacity is to be able to forge exactly the right solution. And he wants to live an intellectual but practical existence, surrounding himself with both thinkers and doers. And when we apply those variables to the formula, we arrive at his point: to make the world a better, fairer place. Simple.

Documentation is commitment.

One of the problems with all this is that we try stuff and we learn stuff, but we never really commit to stuff, which means not much, if any, progress occurs. Sammy Davis, Jr., the Frank Sinatra pal and fellow crooner from the '60s, supposedly once declared: "You always have two choices: your commitment versus your fear."[21] Even when we declare our commitments, they tend to float away because we never write them down. Back to Alison. If she had written her weight loss goal on a little yellow sticky note and stuck that sucker on her bathroom mirror or refrigerator, do you think that might have moved her to try harder? Of course, it would have. Documentation is commitment. And it serves as an accessible reminder of what the hell you're going for and what you've learned along the way. That's why I've asked you to do written exercises at the end of every chapter. No writing, no real commitment, no progress. I can pretty much guarantee it.

I also believe that documentation is critical to affect real learning. I am always amazed at the number of people who seek my counsel, attend my workshops, and listen to my speeches but never write a word down. How could they possibly remember much of anything? The theory of osmotic learning is bull crap. Sure, you might pick up a thing or two, but the lessons really don't stick until you write them down, until you commit both to embracing the newfound under-standing and acting on it.

I guarantee you that if all you do is read this book, without writing down something, you will end up not really learning anything and therefore not changing anything. Documenta-tion is commitment.

So, let's say you've done the work I've prescribed. You've explored. You've sucked it up and tried on new things for size. You've written down the key stuff. And along the way you've felt you, you've seen you respond, you've watched your heart race and your mind accelerate. You're beginning to get an inkling of your P, UC, and NE, and from that, your point. Not a job, not a sofa, but the way you want to be, a world you want to be in, the direction of your True North, the life you want to live. It's time to write that down. Call it a vision statement. Call it whatever the hell you want. Just write it down. Make it short, make it long—it does not matter. Just make it about you, the future you, for you.

Picturing you.

Your point, or your vision statement, does not need to be limited to words. In fact, one of the most powerful point-setting exercises you can do is to create a vision board. It's a collage of handpicked imagery and maybe words that capture your intentions and aspirations. Go buy a large poster board. Start cutting out compelling images from magazines and newspapers. Grab screenshots from places you visit online. Print them out. Sit down one evening with a glass of wine, some scissors, and glue, and make a collage that captures where you want to go. Don't overthink it, just feel it.

Once it's done let it sit around for a while. Try daydreaming those images into a virtual reality. Imagine what that life will be like and what it will feel like. And then work on feeling those feelings and being alert to people and things that reflect your vision board. The more open you are, the more your feelings will emanate toward your desired future and its component parts, and the more everything will align as contributors to your point. Okay, okay, there's a bit of Rhonda Byrne's *The Secret* in all this. And while I don't subscribe to some of her mumbo jumbo, I do believe that visualization leads to realization. So, visualize, please. P.S.: This is also a great exercise for couples to do together. A fun forcing of the future each of you aspires to, separately and together.

It's okay to digitize you, too.

If you're too cool for school for an old-fashioned vision board, set up a separate Instagram page or, hell, why not create a website instead. Not a professional site, not a personal site, but a Self-site. I know, it sounds daunting and many of you are putting up mental "technical roadblocks" right now. But that's silly. The tech part is really easy (SquareSpace, for example). Check out www.chriscolbert.com for one example. Building your site will be easy; the content part will be hard. And when you go to write your "About Me" section, it will hurt your brain. Remember, documentation is commitment. So, when you start writing, you're declaring, and declaring can be unnerving. You'll write multiple drafts and be frustrated. But you'll get there. I have no doubt.

Look motivation straight in the face.

The steps and tasks to find your point really point to the question of motivation. If our imaginary friend Alison really wants to lose weight, is desperate to lose weight, she will set a goal, establish a plan, commit to sacrifice, take on her fears, take on risk, and accomplish her goal. But if she is only half in the game, she won't find the courage to make the sacrifice. She'll talk about losing weight for months, maybe years. She'll eat an extra salad or two when she feels especially guilty, but the number on that scale isn't likely to waver much.

Behavior change is effectively sacrifice, and as shared a chapter back, there are only two motivators of sacrifice: aspiration or desperation. Period. And desperation is the more effective one.

Here's a slightly gross example. Years ago I went to my dentist for teeth cleaning. He admonished me for not flossing. In the spirit of TMI, I have soft gums. Not one cavity but lots of soft gum. I ignored him. Six months later I went back, and this time he said, "Chris, if you don't start flossing, I am going to start cutting [your gums]." I have flossed every day of my life since then. Desperation really works.

(IM: Think about the times in your life that you have been desperate, and how that motivated you to act. Cause yields effect every time.)

So, the key to Lesson #2 is deciding right now that you are desperate to achieve a more fulfilling life. In fact, the rest of this book and whether you get any value out of it at all is entirely dependent on how motivated you are. Motivation is everything.

I recently met with a young woman who just moved to Boston from Russia. An MBA graduate, she is having a hard time finding a job, in large part because her English is not stellar. Her husband runs a small business and they are financially okay, but she wants to find employment. I asked her what she was doing to improve her English. She said she was reading a book a week. I said, "Really?" And she said, "Well, not really, I've been busy." And I said, "Then you are not desperate enough." She wants to find a job, but she does not need to find a job. And there is a huge difference in need versus want. Need is desperation; want is aspiration.

Want tends to fail us at the sacrificial moment, because sacrifice is so damn hard. Need is more effective because, well, we need it. And this is where Maslow once again nailed it. He realized that the foundational needs, the so-called physiological ones of food, warmth, and shelter, inform 90 percent of our behaviors. So, the question for you right now is this: Is your motivation to read this book, to find a way to a better life, based on want or need? If want, beware. If need, move faster.

Are you ready to sacrifice something to get to your point?

Years ago I found myself in a lovely job, with a lovely corner office in a lovely Class A office tower with a really lovely paycheck. And I was miserable. I began to turn up the volume on doing new stuff and concurrently on examining myself. Intensely, constantly watching my reactions to things and people, and how they would impact my mood. What was making me happy? What was making me sad? What was leaving me dazed and half-dead in the water?

What I came to realize was that my greatest joy, my passion, came from creating things. Ideas, images, words, inventions, improvements, anything that was better than what was there before, anything that helped people. I also learned that I had a unique ability to get people excited about a different future, their future, and to realize the full possibility of it. And finally, I realized that I yearned to be in a fully creative, open, intellectual environment that supported my passions, while allowing me to contribute in a meaningful and diverse way. All of this was and is my point. But the question then became whether or not I was willing to sacrifice to achieve it. Was I willing to walk away from a cush gig and a large paycheck in order to get to my point? Turns out I was. Phew.

And the same question applies to you. Are you willing to give something, anything, up to get to your point and to realize your fullest possibility? No pain, no gain. It's true. So, buckle up and let's do this.

Three Things You Should Do Now

1. Start a journal to capture all this stuff, including jotting down what you're willing to sacrifice. Try to write in it every day, even if for three minutes. Write down what you have learned thus far from reading this book and from observing your Self.

2. Start taking a little risk by connecting with new and unfamiliar things, new people, and new experiences. Set a goal of three a week, in any form.

3. Start working on your vision board (or website). Gather images and words that capture the feelings and form of your desired future, your point. Because remember, the point is the point!

you need a map to realize your point

As much as I respect all the self-help writers who have come before me, what blows *my* mind is how most of their books are just collections of good ideas presented without an actionable strategy or framework. And therefore, they're not much help. No framework, no map, no progress. Imagine the gold miners contemplating heading west in America way back when. Wagon? Check. Horses? Check. Whiskey? Check. Map? Nope. The term "circling your wagons" would have ended up meaning something completely different.

Without a strategy, some clear structure, intended milestones, and a map, your ability *and motivation* to achieve your desired point are seriously compromised. Remember, most of the time a hope and a prayer don't get you very far. You may be crystal clear on your destination, but getting there becomes a collection of random acts and delirious stumbles. Without a decent map, you might end up sitting in a snowed-in cabin eating a body part. And along the way you suffer frustration, exhaustion, and occasional bouts of mind-warping melancholy. A good solid map not only provides direction and a dose of sanity but also gives you confidence that you know what to do and what to do next (even if you really don't).

So, the third lesson is this: *You Need a Map to Realize Your Point. Even if your point is clear, if the path is not, you will most likely walk around in circles and eventually give up. Or you won't walk at all. So, make a map, dammit. And here's how.*

The best maps are plotted.

There are maps that depict highways and byways, and then there are maps that point the way (to the point). We're after the latter. And the best maps are plotted. I love the word *plot*. A plot is a scheme, a strategy, a way—the brilliant means and essential milestones that are going to keep you focused on the point while propelling you forward. A massive caveat here: A plot to your point will *not* be perfect, will *not* be exact, and should *not* be fixed. In fact, a sound plot has the capacity to accommodate unforeseen characters, surprising developments, and wholly new opportunities to explore tangential paths and micro-story lines. A solid plot should keep you focused and motivated while allowing your life to unfold in uncertain ways. Because uncertainty is pretty much the only certainty. A plotted map gets you to where you want to be, but not exactly the way you thought. Which makes it all that much more interesting.

Wishful thinking is not a map.

Remember Alison? She was our imaginary friend in Chapter Two who was trying to lose weight. But because she had no point in mind, no specific destination for her weight loss journey, her ability to get "there" was effectively null and void. There was no there there. So, now let's say she read Chapter Two and my powerful and convincing prose (of course) motivated her to establish a point. A goal. A subsequent conversation with her pal Gerry might go like this:

Alison: I am going to lose ten pounds in six weeks.

Gerry: Wow, that seems like a lot in a small amount of time. How are you going to do it? What's your plan?

Alison: I don't have a plan per se. I am just going to watch what I eat and work out a little bit more.

The likelihood that Alison will achieve her goal is slim (pun intended) to none. Hers is not a solid map; there is no plot. There is no strategy; there are no milestones. There's just the hope this will all miraculously work out. Right.

(IM: Contemplate something you've always wanted and how you've wished for it. You didn't actually do anything, you just wished for it. How did that end up?)

So, there's an asterisk to all this. Even if Alison has a plotted map, for example, courtesy of Weight Watchers, the likelihood that she will reach her weight goal *and maintain it* is questionable. In fact, 99 percent of people who follow diet plans and lose weight are back to their original weight within one year. So, what's going on here?

Turns out that as important as plotting is, it's really only 50 percent of the equation. The other 50 percent is making it happen, following the steps, doing the thing, taking action. Another great Mark Twainism comes to mind: *The secret to getting ahead is getting started.*

We're talking behavior modification. And not just any kind of behavior modification, people. The hardest kind: *sustained* behavior modification. The kind that sticks. Whether you are trying to lose weight or attempting to unleash the power of your full creative Self, we're talking about changing your ways for good (for you). And that's the tough part.

So, let's take a wee but important detour to examine why changing our ways is so crushingly hard.

Sacrifice sucks, and the truth hurts.

There are many aspects of our lives that would benefit from conscious plotting, rigorous planning, and sustained implementation. Weight loss is one for sure, but we could also include retirement planning, career planning, and personal health management. Hell, why not include faltering marriages? It turns out the rigorous contemplation, creation, and implementation of plans and actions that would benefit us mightily are mighty hard. And that inability is increasingly universal, of almost epidemic proportion.

We are not rigorous about who we vote for. We are not rigorous about who we marry. We are not rigorous about love or money, about our future, or even about the present day. The vast majority of our decisions and non-decisions are made purely emotionally, without a lick of rigor. Fact-check yourself on this: When was the last time you thoroughly analyzed much of anything? Our growing societal reliance on crude emotion and our alarming lack of rigor is increasingly killing us, literally and figuratively. The existence of "alternative facts" is funnily enough factual proof that we aren't rigorous about much. What the hell.

(IM: Contemplate why exactly you voted for whomever you voted for. How much research and reading did you do, really?)

The problem with rigorous anything is that it is, well, rigorous. And the word rigorous is code for difficult and hard. Rigor requires focus, study, contemplation, and considered decision-making. And who wants to do that? Not me, and most likely not you. It requires looking the truth in the face, acting preventively, and most importantly, being willing to sacrifice stuff we want or want to do for what we really should do.

Think about it.

According to a 2016 GO Banking Rates study, 56 percent of all-American families have $10,000 or less in retirement savings, and 33 percent have zero. Leaving aside for the moment the struggles some families have just meeting their basic needs, why is this happening, particularly when there is no pension system anymore and there are three gazillion financial advisors chomping at the bit to help us all plan? Because to save takes rigor, and it takes sacrifice. It takes a studied effort to understand investment terms like bonds, ETFs, and compound interest. Yum. And it takes a willingness to sacrifice our desire for immediate things like a new Pottery Barn sofa in order to fund our 401(k). New things make us feel good. Money we aren't allowed to use doesn't. We're junkies for junk. So, we don't save. And we don't want to accept the truth of our own mortality; that's depressing. We're going to live forever! Who needs to save? I want what I want, and I deserve it. Right.

Let's examine another one.

Why do 40 percent of marriages in the United States fail? Is it because people fall out of love? Sure, that happens. But I bet the bigger reasons are all of the above: Couples don't confront the truth of what is really going on when things aren't quite right, they don't seek to prevent the problems, and they aren't willing to make sacrifices to save the relationship, even when so much is at stake. And they fundamentally don't want to do the rigorous work. I am but one example, guilty as charged. And when you throw in things like fear of confrontation and of telling the truth, no wonder the marriage industry is on the rocks.

(IM: If you're in a marriage or committed relationship, take a moment here to ponder how hard you both work or don't work at applying rigor (and courage) to the health of your partnership.)

Regardless of the circumstance, if you really want to get to a better place in your life, you need to embrace rigor as a requisite, you need a plot and a plan, and you need the guts to see the truth and make the sacrifices necessary to realize the change you seek. It's basic. And you know what? No amount of my wacky logic is going to motivate you to do this. As I wrote about in Chapter Two, I kinda, sorta wish you an acceptable rock bottom—a rock bottom that hurts but not too much. Rock bottom will make you desperate, and in your desperation, you will find motivation to do the hard work, to make the sacrifices, to embrace the truth, and to work toward prevention versus waiting for the remediation need to smack you in the face.

Absent rock bottom, you will need a steely constitution, a bucket of conviction, and a preternatural willingness to embrace rigor as your friend. These items cannot be found at Home Depot. They can only be found within you.

Map making 101: start with your Balance Sheet.

Assuming you've found your bucket of conviction or some acceptable form of rock bottom, the first step in plotting your map involves taking inventory of what you're after, what you've got to work with, and what you need to worry about. Some percentage of you reading this are now getting cold feet because it sounds like a lot of work. It is. And worse, it's personal. Sorry. But if you want to reach your point, if you want to get to a better life, you have to do crap like this. In fact, according to a study done by Cornell University, the number one attribute of successful entrepreneurs and leaders is, wait, *self-awareness*. Yup.

Knowing your Self, the good and the bad, the strengths and the weaknesses, is essential in your ability to move your Self forward. So, all this time we've been thinking that only self-help gurus believe and say this stuff, and it turns out that the research scientists believe it's true too.

So, think of your Balance Sheet, which I'm about to help you create, as a crisp capture of your Self and the key components that can help you plot your map. But be forewarned. This will take a fair amount of time, contemplation, and writing. There are no pills to pop to get this foundational work figured out. The good news is that if you've done the Chapter Two work, you're almost halfway there. If you haven't (you slug), take a quick trip back to Chapter Two and do that work. And when you get back here, find a large piece of white paper and a fine-tip black Sharpie and start taking inventory of the following Balance Sheet items.

THE STUFF FROM CHAPTER TWO:

Your Point: A good point, an effective and motivating point, is a simple idea or expression that captures the way you want to be and the ultimate Why of your existence, the big hairy audacious outcome you're after. *Mine is to help thousands, maybe even millions, of people realize their full potential, their possibility.*

Your Passion: It's what you love, what you care about, what floats your boat. This is the Why of your stuff. It does *not* have to be complicated. *Mine is to help people, and specifically, to apply creativity and clarity to their personal and professional challenges.*

Your Unique Capacities: This is the One Simple Thing or OST. What's your standout ability/sensibility that defines you? This is the What stuff. What's the simple label that your friends put on you? *My friends, employees, and clients tell me I am uniquely capable of motivating them to see and realize new possibilities by listening well, working hard to understand their realities, and then helping them craft a simple but effective path to a different place. Kind of what I am trying to do with you and this book, absent the listening part, of course.*

Your Desired Nature of Your Existence: This is the How you want to be. Remember, this is the murkiest of the three, but it really is the most important. This is a declaration of the kind of life you want to live as measured by the interactions within it. *My desired Nature of Existence is to surround myself with honesty, intimacy of thought and heart, and creative seekers who want to engage in meaningful, compelling ways. And an occasional lovely glass of wine.*

AND NOW THE NEW STUFF:

The Unwritten Rules of You (Current): This inventory component is a personalized version of a concept first captured in a book called *The Unwritten Rules of the Game*. Written by a management consultant named Peter Scott-Morgan, his thesis is that all organizations are guided not by formalized values and principles, but by the unwritten rules— belief systems that have informally evolved over time. Having run several and consulted with hundreds of companies, I buy what Pete's selling. And I believe it applies to people as well.

I bet it's the unwritten, unspoken rules of us that define our actions and behaviors more than anything. Our unwritten rules are unwritten because they are a subconscious derivation from a multitude of sources, ranging from genetic disposition to family legacy behaviors to personal experience. We don't wake up one day and say, "Hey, I think I'm going to put together my unwritten rules!" They just are.

So, what are your unwritten rules? The good, the bad, and maybe even the ugly? My past unwritten rules, when I was that intense, closed-off automaton of a man were:

The good: Don't let anyone down.
The bad: Avoid intimacy at all costs.
The ugly: Control everything to avoid risk.

Since these rules are not written, not formally established, you may be scratching your head regarding how exactly to capture them. Totally legit. I got to mine after seven years of therapy. Assuming you want to fast track your discovery and need some clues, try asking your Self the following questions:

What are the unstated don'ts in my/our birth family? For example, what do Mom and/or Dad never want to hear, see, or talk about? It's okay to ask your siblings this question, although not asking may be an unwritten rule itself!

In my relationships with people of the opposite sex, what have I been hesitant to express?

What am I most afraid of?

There are scores more of good questions to put out there. The key is to start asking.

(IM: Ask your Self why you hate doing this work? What are you actually afraid of?)

The Unwritten Rules of You (Desired): So, the desired unwritten rules are, well, your desired unwritten rules. Their definition and declaration are a capture of your commitment to your evolution and should be reflective of or somewhat connected to your point. So, if you could rewrite your rules (and you can) to better reflect how you want to be and the ways you want to behave, what would you want the rules to be? Try keeping them to the top three because any more will either diffuse the power of this picture or just confuse you.

My current unwritten rules, which used to be my desired ones (thank you, psychotherapists and friends) are:

The good: Try to help everyone without judgment.
The better: Be honest and open-hearted, always.
The best: Remember it's all good, even the crappy crap.
The still slightly ugly: Control everything as much as possible.

But wait, that's four rules! Right. And they don't perfectly match up with my old rules. What the hell? The reason is this: This stuff is not a perfect prescription. If you want one of those, shut this book and head to your local pharmacy. This is a framework to get you to think differently and hopefully motivate you to do something differently. And the existence of the slightly ugly rule reflects the fact that these rules are a work in progress. Your rules are going to change, driven either by your own evolution or the life forces that you will inevitably encounter.

What's important is that you recognize their existence and you work toward establishing a healthier set that you learn to live by and that propels you toward your point. The final proof that things don't always line up perfectly: You actually have to write down your unwritten rules, which makes them written unwritten rules. Geez.

Essential Risks: This inventory item is a little more challenging to define, but arguably it's one of the most important ones. The question is twofold: What are the risks you are worried about in taking this journey, and what are the risks that you realize you must take to get to your desired destination? *The risks I worried about way back when I decided I wanted to change were the loss of friends, the inability to make new friends, the loss of my business, the loss of my children, the*

54

loss of everything I valued. . . . The risks I realized I had to take were the risk of losing everything and the risk of exposing my limitations. If I did not take these risks, I would remain stuck, surrounded by all I valued but without the ability to fully realize and contribute to that value. I knew that I had to risk everything, including my pride, to realize everything, including me.

Low-Hanging Opportunities: Unless you've been skim reading, which is entirely possible, you now know that the likelihood of realizing your point and a better life will be determined by the level of motivation you bring to the journey. And one way to find some quick motivation is by acting on what I call low-hanging opportunities, a slightly modified version of a bucket list. These are things you have always wanted to do, the people you have always wanted to connect with, and the endeavors that have been circling around your brain and heart forever—endeavors that are reflective of the Self you really want to be. With your newfound enlightenment, you now realize that the only thing that stands between you and checking these things off the list is that insidious little bastard known as fear. I suggest you suck it up (read Chapter Four) and take full advantage of these low-hanging opportunities to realize your true Self ASAP. One of the biggest benefits of going after these in-your-face opportunities is that you'll likely conquer them, showing your Self quite quickly that the degree of difficulty associated with change, big or small, is not as fearful as you feared, and once you get some positive momentum going, it makes the next set of newfound actions and behaviors a little easier. It's a bit like priming the pump. A little dribble at first will become a torrent. *My low-hanging opportunities back then included learning how to cook, starting my first business, and trying to tell my girlfriend how I actually felt about myself and my life, and her. All three were right before my eyes and completely riddled with a multitude of fears. But I did them, and in doing so, found more motivation.*

Relevant Weaknesses: The last line item in your Balance Sheet requires some courage to complete. Actually, all of this requires courage to complete because depicting your Self in black and white is like taking off your clothes in the middle of a business meeting. The question is, what are the big, mondo, personal weaknesses that really stand in the way of you moving forward? What are you most afraid of? Or worried about? Why do you choose to not do what you want to do? *My big weakness was the incessant need for self-protection. I realized that I could not engage the world, engage others, engage my own kids, or even engage my Self as long as my arms were wrapped tightly around my body and my heart was closed.*

Okay, so what have you created? It's a Balance Sheet where the assets clearly outweigh the liabilities. Or maybe not! But that's okay because all this will change. Your Balance Sheet is an ever-shifting view of how well you're doing, feeling, and achieving your march toward a better life. As the content will change, so, too, will the weighting as your plot unfolds and you make progress toward your point.

Your Balance Sheet is also a cheat sheet for you to use as you develop your plot and your plan. How so? Each of the components of your Balance Sheet should either inform your plot, inform your strategy, and/or contribute to the formation of a milestone. Your plot should lie at the intersection of leveraging your assets (Passions, Unique Capacities) and mitigating your liabilities (Current Unwritten Rules and Relevant Weaknesses). Or more simply said: What can you do to take advantage of your strengths and interests while reducing the impact of your limitations and not-so-helpful ways?

You can also think about all this like Richard Rumelt, a UCLA Professor and author of a book titled *Good Strategy Bad Strategy*.[22] He defines strategy (plotting) as problem solving with three parts: diagnosis that defines the nature of the challenge, a guiding policy for dealing with the challenge, and coherent actions to implement the guiding policy. So, your Balance Sheet is a form of diagnosis, a source of guiding policy, and a wellspring of ideas on the actions you may want to take to realize that policy (in particular, revisit your low-hanging opportunities).

When I did my Balance Sheet years ago, it helped me come up with what was effectively a plotted map. I called it "My Intentions," and it consisted of three buckets of outcomes, milestones, and the plot to get there. Three columns on a single page of paper with these words:

Plot: Find a role and a lifestyle that allow me to lead, create, and communicate and take risk every day. Open my Self up to everything and everybody. Observe and learn every step of the way. Oh, and forgive my Self.

Milestones: Formalize mentoring role, get a job in the education sector, become content with being alone, establish trust with my kids, write a book.

Outcome: To help thousands, maybe millions, of people realize their full potential.

Okay, so even if you don't want to do the work to turn your Balance Sheet into a plot and the beginning of a map, it should be helpful to have this picture of you, right? Pop singer Shakira gets it, because in an interview with *The Guardian* she shared, "I just think that it's very helpful to have a map of your psyche, because when you have a map, you know where to go."[23]

You know where to go. Absent categorization, declaration, and documentation, we simply cannot get anywhere. We cannot realize our point or any of the milestones between where we are and where we want to be. Now, assuming you do want to do this plot-your-map thing, you have a choice: What kind of map do you want to make?

The perfect map is in the mind of the mapper.

So, it turns out there is no perfect map or plotting model. That would be like thinking that psychotherapy should be one size fits all.

I know this is upsetting. After all, we live in a panacea-fixated society! We believe little blue pills will cure pretty much anything. Well, there ain't no little blue pill. Everybody is different, which means every map should be different. As an example, in my work at the Harvard Innovation Labs I got asked daily what the right sequence of steps is, what the right formula is, and what the approach is to create a successful startup. If I knew the answer to that, I'd be writing a different book. My response to those basic questions was always an obtuse and maybe even metaphysical, "It depends."

It depends on where you start, the point you want to realize, the resources you have, and where you want to end up. In other words, it depends on the assets and liabilities in your balance sheet. It also depends on factors outside of your control and a bunch within.

Map-making is variable and highly personal. I don't really care what kind of map you create, only that you create a map. You simply will not reach your point without one. Take a second and Google "Personal Life Planning." You'll get thousands of types of maps. Just pick one. I've offered my three favorite options below.

But whatever map you pick, use a pencil.

Seriously. In his 2015 commencement speech at Rutgers University-Camden, rocker Jon Bon Jovi said, "Life is a long, bumpy road, but that makes for an exciting ride. Choose a direction and if the road turns — turn! If there is a fork in the road – take it! It's ok to map out your future — but do it in pencil."[24] Exactly. Using a pencil is a way of recognizing that things will change, your aspirations will change, and even your point might change.

Now you may be asking yourself, "Well, what's the point of a map if everything will change?" Valid question. Perhaps the biggest point of a map is that it will motivate you to actually do something. Documentation really is commitment, and the physical presence of a map will remind you that there is still work to do, and the work will get you what you want. A good map also helps you get over the feeling of being overwhelmed by the task of getting from where you are to where you want to be. It forces you to break down this mountain of fear and questions, and results in a far more accessible view of how to get there.

And if I may make a suggestion, mapping something, even if not perfectly plotted, is better than doing nothing at all. So, it doesn't matter how much you erase, redraw, or redefine the point or the plot. Just by doing it, you are doing something.

So now, for those who want some examples of mapping approaches, I give you my favorite three.

One option: The Startup Road Map.

This is less a directive map and more a framework to translate your Balance Sheet into a sequential proposition that you can monitor and adjust as your path unfolds. It's called the entrepreneurial startup road map as crafted by Michael Skok, a venture capitalist pal of mine. Michael's mostly linear depiction of the entrepreneurial journey, with some creative license applied by me, kinda goes like this:

Stage I: *Ideation, elation, and abject fear.* The determination of a potential destination, your Point, and your decision to embark on this journey. Yikes!

Stage II: *Contemplation, exploration, and creation.* The formation of the intended product (in your case, the intended person). This is your work on Passion, Unique Capacities, and Nature of Existence. Be bold; be honest. Try to bring the pieces together as one cogent, composite view.

Stage III: *Validation or invalidation.* The realization of the MVP (Minimum Viable Product) and whether or not it is appealing. So, this is your Minimum Viable Person. Is this new trajectory working for you? Are your Low-Hanging Fruit opportunities happening? Are you embracing the Essential Risks and minimizing your Relevant Weaknesses? How does it feel?

Stage IV: *The pivot.* Not always but often, the decision to change course based on MVP findings and market factors. In your case, if the path or places on it are not feeling good, take a hard left. Or plot a new map.

Stage V: *More validation or invalidation.* Hopefully the former, or another pivot is in order.

Stage VI: *Repeatability.* This is where the newfound actions, behaviors, and decision-making ways start becoming more familiar within your life.

Stage VII: *The unexpected near-death experience.* Okay, this is less a sequential stage and more a cruel likelihood that will happen somewhere along the way. This is when something unexpected happens that completely throws you off your path and has you questioning your intentions, convictions, and the map itself. Nice. It's a test, and you can pass it. Just look it in the face, embrace it for its learning gift, and shove that sucker in the trunk of the car and get back on the road.

Stage VIII: *Rebound and acceleration.* The shock of the near-death experience turns into clarity and a bit of an adrenalin rush. All of a sudden, the new way, the new you, is clicking.

Chris Colbert

Your Point looks achievable, your Passions are being realized, your Unique Capacities are being put to use, and the Nature of Your Existence is fundamentally the nature of your existence! So, what now? *Crank it up!* Now is the time to pour more gasoline into your engine (see Lesson #4, Self-Love Is the Accelerant) and hit the pedal to get further, faster. Woo-hoo!

Stage IX: *Scalability and predictability.* This is when you turn the learnings and intermittent adventures of your new life into a sustainable proposition. It's when the dream you had is now your central reality. Your decisions are consistent, your priorities are without question, and your choices are the right choices that honor you and contribute to your point. Predictability is not boring; it simply means you can count on this way of living as being the way you live. Exactly.

As noted earlier, while this approach is called a road map, it's really just a depiction of how this could all unfold. If you like the idea, think of using it as an active, intentional journal. Find another really large piece of white paper, even a poster board, whip out your Sharpie, draw the Stages as columns, and begin filling in what you know, what you seek, and so on. And keep updating it with accomplishments, setbacks, new learning, revised thinking—anything that will help you form and reform both the destination and the path to it. Make it part map, part journal, and part scoreboard of your effort to evolve you.

Or do this.

Try a different route.

Now for something completely conceptual. Applying the startup sequential thing to yourself has the benefit of being, well, sequential. But is all this really sequential? And what if you're not a sequential thinker? So, here's a decidedly less overt and less linear approach, one that may appeal to the big

61

thinkers or the folks who don't want to be hemmed in. I call it the Quadrant System. And it too requires a large white piece of paper and a fine-point Sharpie. It works like this:

Create a large 2-x-2 matrix, as large as you can make it. (A black Sharpie on your off-white bedroom wall can make for a compelling visual and daily reminder.) Draw the 2-x-2 matrix like this:

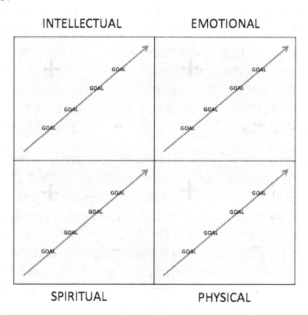

Think of each quadrant or box as its own mapping territory. Now draw an arrow from the lower left corner of each box to the upper right corner. Then start filling it in, using the material you created from your Balance Sheet. The asset (+) stuff should go above each arrow, and the liability (–) stuff below. The goal is to create four distinct but connected maps, each with time-based milestones, a.k.a. goals, for each of the dimensions of you, goals that once realized will add up to your big Point, your Point B. If I went back in time and used this kind of map on my Self, with the Balance Sheet content as shared, my Emotional quadrant would include my old Unwritten Rules as liabilities, my desired Unwritten Rules as assets, and the four following time-based milestones to get to the big Emotional goal of loving my Self:

Find a great therapist—2002
Get better at sharing needs with partner—2003
Make more close friends—2005
Pick courage over fear consistently—2007

The underlying idea here is that in order to realize the Why of you, your Point, your Passions, and your Unique Capacities, you must work to evolve your Self on every dimension. The journey before us is necessarily a journey of mind, heart, spirit, and body, and we can only get to our desired destination if each dimension is enriched and fully realized. I know that sounds like a little mumbo jumbo, but how about this bit of brilliance from the revered scientist, Oakley Ray, Professor Emeritus of Psychology, Psychiatry, and Pharmacology at Vanderbilt University who once wrote:

"According to the mind–body or biopsychosocial para-digm, which supersedes the older biomedical model, there is no real division between mind and body because of networks of communication that exist between the brain and neurological, endocrine and immune systems."[25]

What he said. Everything is connected. In order to realize the full potential of you, you need to realize every dimension of you. It's that simple.

Or try mine.

If neither of these map options float your boat, there is always a third: mine.

It's the map my wife Kate and I made last summer to chart our next ten years. It's ridiculously simple, which may be its strength.

Imagine a large white piece of paper...I know. Seriously, it's a piece of paper with an elongated spiral in blue pencil going from lower left to upper right. Within each loop is the year (1, 3, 5, 10). The space between the loops captures the big things, such as finish this book and create a learning community, with the loop titles capturing some other life changes, for example, visit Berlin, complete addition, and live elsewhere.

The map sits on my desk. I am aware of it every day. And that is its power and value. Changing a situation first requires awareness of the situation and then the desire to change it. The map reminds me of what we are at the end and the journey to get there. It serves as motivation and reinforcement that perhaps all this really isn't that hard. Somehow the confusing view of the future has been magically distilled down to eight or nine tasks or milestones. Bingo! And its sheer existence on an energetic level increases the likelihood that some, if not all, of this stuff might actually happen. If you buy this (which I, of course, do) read *The Secret* by Rhonda Byrne.

Documentation is commitment, right?

Hopefully, you now get that the type of map and the particular plot you make do not matter. I repeat, they do not matter. What matters is documentation of a plan (in pencil), any plan, because that signals commitment and serves as motivation. My only caveat is this: Avoid tons of detail. Don't attempt a blow by blow, because things are going to change. You are going to change. And that is the point, right? And as you begin to plot your plot and map your map, try to get your head around the following three truisms:

There are no straight lines.

Nope. Not a one. Because there are too many variables at play, too many dimensions of you involved, and simply too much complexity to be able to achieve the simplicity of a straight line. As I have hammered since Chapter One, the evolution of you and the realization of your full potential is not about the flicking of a switch. It's more like rewiring the circuitry of a jet fighter while in midair, in a dogfight during a hailstorm. It's hard, it's scary, even nauseating. It's fraught with mild electric shocks and maybe even shrapnel. And it is decidedly not straight. So, don't make a straight-line map. Plan for detours, excursions, random off-roading, and an occasional breakdown. And you're going to find that you learn as much or more from the side road adventures as you do from the main thoroughfare.

Embrace the highwaymen.

In the spirit of beating a metaphor to death, know that along your journey there will be highwaymen out to carjack you. Really.

Well, not *really*.

But there *are* all sorts of forces at work to dissuade you from continuing forward. Friends or even partners who don't like what your map contains (and what it might mean to their relationship with you), money voices that tell you to avoid risk, and even legacy notions that try to convince you that this new direction is antithetical to your core. It's essential that you see these influences as legitimate and loving, and then explain to them, whoever they are, that as much as you respect their concerns, your desire to get to a better place, to innovate your life, is simply more important.

Forward progress is more important than perfection.

Or as Voltaire once penned ". . . the best is the enemy of the good."[26] Part of the reason people don't take actions to improve their lot in life is because they hide in the belief that they need a perfect plan and a perfect outcome. Seeking perfection effectively and ironically becomes one of the primary reasons for failure to even get out of the starting blocks. So please, put perfect aside. What matters is forward progress. When you combine a plotted map, a clear point, and forward progress, you almost can't help but experience accomplishment, even if it's painfully slow. And from accomplishment comes satisfaction and the source material for more motivation to propel you toward the next step, loop, activity, or whatever on your map.

And then the magical thing happens: You achieve momentum and this whole arduous process becomes a whole lot easier. I promise.

The author George Ella Lyon said it pretty well in her novel, *Holding on to Zoe*: "I just know when I quit looking to other people for directions, I found my own map."[27]

<u>Three Things You Should Do Now</u>

1. Complete your Balance Sheet. It won't take more than an hour over a cup of tea or two.

2. Pick a Low-Hanging Opportunity off your list and do it. Doesn't matter what it is, how big or small. Unless it's illegal, in which case you're on your own.

3. Doodle a map. Either one of the ones shared or your own. Assuming you have done the vision boarding exercise from Chapter Two, stick that in front of you, and start creating a map that's pointed toward there. Plot some paths and potential milestones. Document, document, document. Don't overthink this stuff. And use a pencil with an eraser.

self-love is the accelerant

A re you still with me? Then how about an annoying pop quiz?

Actually, there's just one run-on question: Do you get that innovating your life is a must, that you have to establish your point to realize a better life, and that a plotted map would sure come in handy? If not, go back to Chapter One. Seriously.

For extra credit: Do you accept that adhering to the first three lessons in this book is actually pretty straightforward, assuming the existence of one big thing: a sufficient level of your own mildly desperate motivation. You and I both know the real issue is not the challenge of you understanding this stuff, it's actually you doing it. Hell, if everyone just did it, the self-help book industry would collapse. I'd be out of work.

We also covered the idea of motivation and behavior modification being fueled either by desperation (remember acceptable rock bottom?) or aspiration (rare, but it does happen). So, there's another critical factor, and it can make all the difference in your world. It's based on a simple observation: The ability to live a better life, the ability to stick to your plan to achieve your point, will be significantly expedited by how well you understand you, feel you, and most importantly, love you. I call it Self-Love. And if you don't believe me, how about Lucille Ball, the quite brilliant slapstick comedic star from the '60s who once said in all seriousness, "Love yourself first and everything else falls into line. You really have to love yourself to get anything done in this world."[28]

So, if you choose to ignore everything else I have shared, okay. It hurts slightly, but okay. Just don't ignore Lucy and Lesson #4. *Self-Love Is the Accelerant. Unconditional love of Self, the dark and the light, is the freeing agent that allows us to more readily see the truth, share the truth, take the risks, and make the sacrifices in order to achieve our point.*

Self-Love enables us to be intimate with ourselves, with our loved ones, and with the world. Such universal intimacy is the greatest accelerant of the journey toward our point and a better life because it serves as constant reward and an effective reminder of why we're doing all this to begin with. And it gives us the courage to take on all the demons. By realizing Self-Love, we gain another powerful form of motivation that will keep us marching forward, regardless of the fears and foes that will inevitably appear.

Self-Love is an enabler, a motivator, and a reminder. But most importantly it is an accelerant. And now that you have a few of the other lessons under your (seat) belt, it's time to hit the gas.

First things first: Self-Love is not self-esteem.

According to Merriam-Webster, god love her, self-esteem is all about having confidence in one's ability. That's a good thing, because it makes interacting with others a whole lot more pleasant. In a low self-esteem state, every conversation has the capacity to conjure up sweaty palms or worse. Been there, done that.

Self-Love is a good thing too, but it's different. It's more of a way of being and is necessarily all about you. Having solid Self-Love means having the capacity to always be present and to not just hear your heart but to follow it. It means loving both the wonder of you *and* the hairy warts. Gross. It means believing that anything is possible while you're also hugging your limitations. Self-Loving accepts that a life well lived begins and ends with unconditional acceptance of every part of your person, and a full-on embrace of all the ups and downs of your life as they appear. A Self-Loving person is open to lifelong learning, connected to his or her passions and interests, and most importantly, not afraid to put anything about their Self on the table. And all that makes adhering to the other *This Is It* lessons a whole lot easier and their realization a whole lot more effective.

Think about it. When your Self-Love is alive and well:

- Embracing that you must evolve (Lesson #1) shifts from being an intellectual exercise to a matter of the heart, which can make it more tangible. Instead of being motivated to evolve because you know you should, you are motivated to evolve because your Self deserves it. If you love you, of course you want to evolve you. No debate.

- Determining your point (Lesson #2) becomes much easier. High Self-Love correlates with high self-awareness, which includes an understanding of your Passions, your Unique Capacities, and your Desired Nature of Existence. When you love you, you know you, and the more clearly you know where you want to go and how you want your life to go.

- You will be less inclined to dread the task of completing your balance sheet and subsequently contemplating and documenting a plotted map (Lesson #3). And you'll also have less dread about reading the rest of this book. Bonus.

The concept of loving Self is simple, right? But it's not that easy, and here's why.

Humans are needy things.

We're really needy. Our actions, perceptions, and perspectives are largely a function of how we feel relative to other people, and specifically how well our needs are being met. Abraham Maslow, a psychologist from the '50s (and my hero), got it exactly right when he hypothesized his now famous "Hierarchy of Need." My twist on his gist is this:

Most Homo Sapiens are deep down inside fearful, thumb-sucking, blanket-hugging, sniveling little kids. Desperately, even if subconsciously, seeking to ensure that our primal needs for food, shelter, comfort, and love will be met. As long as we fear not having little creature comforts, we cannot realize the highest level of need state: Self-Actualization. As long as we are fixated on matters of subsistence, of control, of risk reduction, and of getting validation from others, we cannot realize the full potential of our Self. We cannot realize our point. It makes sense, right? If our daily existence is consumed by worry and fear about not having our basic needs met, there is no way in hell we will find our way to heaven, a.k.a. our point.

Another way to think about this is that every thought we have and every action we take is first put through a subconscious filter of need. And that our resulting action or thought is modified to ensure that our primal needs are met, even if those needs are based on fear and are downright silly. As an example, let's say you and I go to a cocktail party together. When we arrive, we don't recognize a soul. Now examine what's going on inside you. For all your sophistication and seeming bravado, you are reverting to your primal state, with your reptilian brain kicking in and sending fear signals flooding into your frontal lobe. You are afraid of being exposed, of the threat of strangers, and perhaps of not being accepted. We call it being "shy," but it's really being afraid of the unknown. I saw this day in and day out at the Harvard Innovation Labs. Some of the brightest, most confident students in the world showed up every day and, even with my constant encouragement to connect with each other, were simply afraid to put their hands out and say hello.

Silly, and universal.

(IM: Think about your interactions and decisions of late. Ponder the why of them, and how you processed the information and choices through your need filter. You did, right?)

The need for the comfort of validation is perhaps the most nagging of these really basic needs. We eschew the idea of being judged and yet seek positive judgment constantly. What's that about? The need to be accepted and approved by others is the biggest inhibitor of each of us thinking and acting in ways that support us, honor us, and enable us to move forward. It's effectively the opposite of Self-Love. And it is baked into our culture. Does the phrase "Keeping up with the Joneses" ring a bell? Everywhere you look you will see people taking actions to ensure they get direct or indirect validation from others. How many likes did your last Facebook post get? Why exactly do 90 percent of women dye their hair? Why do guys like fast cars?

Validation and its cousin Comparison are insidious forces and addictive, toxic needs that get in the way of us really living our lives the way we want to live them. And sadly, there are a bunch more.

There is much noise in our machine.

Whaaa, whaaa, whaaa. The noise comes in many forms. The voices in our heads, the noise outside, it all fuzzies up our capacity to see clearly, to think purely, to live freely, and to love ourselves unconditionally. Take a moment and contemplate this. What voices do you hear right now? Perhaps the voice of someone you admire, that you wish would admire you more. Perhaps the voice of the past, of regret, of guilt, or shame. Or how about the voice of doubt, the one that yammers at you every day, "Are you really good enough? Are you deserving? Are you worthy?" How about the voice that is telling you right now that you already know this stuff and don't need to do the work?

Right. You do know this stuff. And you do need to do the work. Sorry, pal.

There are all kinds of noises and voices we conceive and perceive, none actually real but all quite present in our head. And they all get in the way of us being able to listen to and love our Self and, as a consequence, change our lot in life and get to our point.

The most incessant, annoying, and disabling voice is the voice I and other contemplative folk refer to as the voice of the Shadow Child. Derived in part from seminal work by the eminent Swiss psychiatrist Carl Jung (and my guardian angel friend Melissa Yahia), the idea is that each of us has a child within us who is needy, whiney, and even obnoxious on occasion. Or in my case, often. And our Shadow Child lives in constant fear. No amount of chicken fingers is going to quell this child's appetite for anxiety.

My Shadow Child is named Jarod (long story). Note the present tense. The little bastard's still around. Jarod was always telling me I couldn't, or I shouldn't, and reminding me that self-protection was my number one job. For most of my life Jarod ran things, informed my Unwritten Rules, created the noise, and served up the desperate needs that thwarted my ability to love me and from that realize me. Jarod did everything he could to avoid intimacy and to maintain control. He was scared, which meant I was scared. He was the one wanting to hug the wall at the cocktail party. He was the one who was afraid to look in the mirror and ask the hard questions. He was the one who was expert at denial and delusion. Does any of this sound familiar? It wasn't until I realized that Jarod, while a part of me, was not *me*, my Self, that I was able to quiet his voice and turn down the noise. I learned how to listen to him without allowing his fears to dominate my feelings and thoughts.

Whether you like it or not, you have a Shadow Child. That's not actually bad news. It's just important information. I'll explain how you can get your Shadow Child and the rest of the voices to quiet down a little bit later. But first let's go a little deeper into why Self-Love is such a powerful accelerant on your journey toward a better life.

Letting go gets you going.

Perhaps paradoxically, Self-Love is less about finding ways to fulfill your needs and more about letting many of them go, whether primal or Pottery Barn. And that is tantamount to letting go of Ego. If, as the Buddha once declared, "Ego is the cause of all suffering," the inverse is true: No Ego is the cause of all non-suffering. Or said another way, Self-Love is the cause of all worthwhile gain.

Ego is what creates fear, unhealthy wants, those crazy doom loops of despair, addictions, and more. The little bastard is also essential to our survival, because without it we would probably walk off cliffs or forget to eat. However, while a critical facet of our being, Ego is not us. Self is who we really are. As Eckhart Tolle writes in his global bestseller *The Power of Now,*

> "As long as the Egoic mind is running your life, you cannot truly be at ease; you cannot be at peace or fulfilled except for brief intervals when you obtained what you wanted, when a craving has been fulfilled. Since the Ego is a derived sense of self (and not Self), it needs to identify with external things. It needs to be both defended and fed constantly."[29]

Ego, the ravenous source of insatiable need, is akin to a tapeworm. It's eating you from the inside out. So, cut it out, or at least cut it in half.

And when you do, you will be released. Really, you will. And in that release, you will realize the strength and determination to evolve, the capacity to establish your point and purpose and the motivation to follow your map. I know I sound like Tony Robbins here, but it's true. You will be readier to choose courage over fear, and more willing to take the risks and make the sacrifices necessary to realize your point. You will be able to embrace the wonder of your Self, to fully love your Self, and to realize that Self-Love really is the accelerant that will get you wherever it is you want to go faster—much, much faster. And as a bonus, you will learn wholly new ways of being, thinking, and observing, ways that will fundamentally change your life.

Yes, this all sounds like some Dorothy in ruby red shoes crap. Actually, it is, in this sense: The scarecrow is you. The cowardly lion is you. The tinman is you. Hell, Dorothy is you. Getting to Self-Love is about seeing behind the emerald curtain and realizing that there is only you. And that you are totally worth loving.

Tout ce que je desire est de dans.

Ten plus years ago, I decided to get a tattoo on my right arm. My inside forearm to be exact. Mom was thrilled. I wanted to create a permanent, visible reminder of the most important life lesson that I had learned: the importance of replacing all of my Ego-driven needs with a pure and simple love of my Self, and a recognition that all I really needed to be happy and to achieve the life I wanted to live was already within me. That I need not need external influence, material goods, or the validation of my actions or abilities. That all I needed was my love of me. And that was within me.

That resulted in the phrase "All that I desire is within," which then got rendered in hacked French: *"Tout ce que je desire est de dans"* on my arm in cursive. Why French, you might ask? Because the way of the French, their focus on depth, expression, and passion (if not their GDP) has always called to me. Bon jour.

Intimacy is all.

Self-Love begins with letting go of Ego, the neediness, the fear, and the noise and then replacing them with intimacy. Intimacy first with Self, intimacy with loved ones, intimacy with the world. The textbook definition of intimacy points toward the idea of emotional closeness and a very private relationship. My definition is slightly different. Intimacy to me is the capacity to remove all barriers between Self and another (including Self) to achieve deep connection of mind, heart, and soul. It is a capacity fueled by love, built on a foundation of honesty, and intended without want, other than to deeply connect with and care for the other. It is a capacity that eschews fear out of desire to achieve that connection. I know this might sound mushy. But it's true.

The sad irony is that most people have an easier time being intimate with acquaintances than they do with loved ones or themselves. Let's call this "The Bartender Effect." According to Dr. Margaret Paul, a PhD and recognized expert in relationships, "Many people have two major fears that may cause them to avoid intimacy: the *fear of rejection* (of losing the other person), and the *fear of engulfment* (of being invaded, controlled, and losing oneself)."[30]

Dammit, we're back to primal fear again. Are you detecting a pattern?

So, crazy as this is, it's easier to tell an almost stranger your deepest, darkest desires and fears than it is your husband, wife, or parent because you don't care about losing a stranger and your relationship with him or her is but a moment in time. My first marriage was a perfect case of how a lack of intimacy can kill a good thing. We were two people who genuinely cared for each other, but we were paralyzed in our ability to be intimate, to tell the truth, and to share desires, fears, wants— anything other than the domestic news. So, as time went by, we drifted further and further apart until it was just too much. And then it was over.

(IM: Got intimacy?)

This same scenario applies to intimacy with Self. Many of us are quite adept at ignoring our truth, suppressing our desires, and being unwilling to simply acknowledge what we are, how we feel, and what we want. Introspection 'R' Not Us. Particularly us men. And because of that we drift further and further apart from our Self and from those around us. And then it is over.

Intimacy with your Self involves several stages of development, from seeing Self truthfully and understanding Self to embracing Self in full (the good, bad, and ugly) and being able to observe and evolve Self as you journey forward. But the most compelling part may actually be being intimate with others. When you approach a conversation with someone in a state of Self-Love, from the heart, without fear, with candor and genuine empathy for the other, when you leave Ego in the closet and only seek connection, the conversation is no longer just a conversation. It is a profound transfer of meaning and a wonderful reminder of what it means to be human.

A true story: Eight years ago, a woman I had never met contacted me for some advice regarding her struggling startup business. We got together at a coffee shop a few days later. The obligatory small talk quickly moved into candor, with my sharing my tale of loss, of fear, and of learning to love my Self. The candor and empathy I exhibited gave her the courage to respond with her own tale and the terrible reveal that she was contemplating suicide. In twenty minutes, we went from being complete strangers to being completely connected. That is the power and importance of intimacy. That is the power and importance of Self-Love. And don't worry, she's in a much better place today.

You cannot love others without first loving your Self.

I really believe this to be true. And apparently so did the psychologist Erich Fromm, who wrote about it in his book *The Art of Loving*. His view, decidedly more scientific than mine, was this:

> ". . . respect for one's own integrity and uniqueness, love for and understanding of one's own Self, cannot be separated from respect and love and understanding for another individual. The love of my own Self is inseparably connected with the love for any other being."[31]

My more ground-level spin is that absent Self-Love, your love for another is put through that filter of need, with fear and doubt distorting all the inbound and outbound signals. Absent Self-Love, it's quite likely your Shadow Child is doing too much of the talking and convincing you to hold back, to omit, to not ask, to stay on guard. Knowing and loving Self intimately enables you to see you as others see you. It enables you to receive their concerns and criticisms in an open versus defensive stance. It also enables you to receive their compliments without deflection.

Take a moment to think about how most people respond to praise: "Oh, it was nothing." "Oh, it was nothing" is a way of saying we don't deserve it. We are not worthy. We are not lovable. Self-Love enables you to receive, to hear, and to be heard without noise, confusion, and deflection. It enables you to love and be loved without condition.

This simple precept underlies why so many pending marriages are pretty much destined to fail. Instead of both parties loving Selves and approaching their union with hearts wide open, ready for intimacy, they show up on the big day slightly broken, with Ego standing in as the best man or maid of honor, a dowry full of needs, and an unspoken hope that the other person can fix them. And they can't. To add insult to an already tenuous situation, they are both afraid of telling each other the truth. They're screwed. The only marriages that really work are the ones made up not of two halves but two holes. And the only way to get whole, to fall in love with Self, is to do the work. Here are some steps.

Embrace your Balance Sheet.

Assuming you read Chapter Three and did what I told you to do, you have a Balance Sheet sitting somewhere around your home. And on that Balance Sheet are four-line items that are really important to get your head around in order to begin falling in love with your Self. The two biggies are your current Unwritten Rules and your desired Unwritten Rules. You've got to get laser focused on how you are versus how you want to be. The Unwritten Rule work should help you get there. Remember mine?

CURRENT (BEFORE)
The good: Don't let anyone down.
The bad: Avoid intimacy at all costs.
The ugly: Control everything to avoid risk.

DESIRED (AFTER)
The good: Try to help everyone without judgment.
The better: Create in some form, every day.
The best: Remember it's all good, even the crappy crap.
The still slightly ugly: Control is hard to completely give up.

The task is not to look at this stuff as positive or negative but rather as lovable. All of it. I know that's going to be hard, but it's key. A big part of this journey to Self-Love is about acceptance and forgiveness. If you hold up your not-so-niceties as negatives, if you don't let go of the sadness and the regrets, you'll never be free to really love, yourself or anyone else.

One of the most common Unwritten Rules that holds people back is the rule "Worry about everything." People's worry and fears are like snake venom. Paralysis within seconds, death to follow. For the first forty years of my life I worried about everything, from the peeling paint on the garage doors to the possibility of the next Great Depression. It froze me in place. Defrosting took a lot of work, but it was triggered by reading an interview with the Dalai Lama who said, paraphrased, "There are two kinds of worry in the world: the worry you can do something about, in which case you should do something about it, and the worry you can't do anything about, in which case you shouldn't worry about it." Exactly. If worry is one of your Unwritten Rules, take a moment to create a two-column list, the Can Worries versus the Can't Worries. And then start working on letting the latter go.

Now take a look at your Relevant Weaknesses line item. The drill is pretty much the same. Love them because you probably can't easily leave them. But start contemplating how to let them go too.

Lastly, let's take another look at some of the Low-Hanging Opportunities. If you did some of the homework from Chapter Three and actually took advantage of one or two of these, you have most probably felt some goodness from the exercise. Maybe you've felt accomplishment, pride, possibly even joy. And in taking the actions you have always wanted to take but didn't, you are both loving your Self and creating some motivational momentum. Turns out that stepping out of your comfort zone is actually fun!

Some other to-dos to help you fall in love with you:

Observe.

To find Self-Love, you have to remove your Self from yourself and observe what's really going on. As long as you are intertwined with the child, with the Ego, consumed by the voice inside and the noise around you, you won't be able to really see, understand, or feel. So, practice rising above your presence to establish an out-of-body view of you. I know this sounds weird and maybe even creepy, but it's critical. You have to be able to watch your words, decisions, actions, and interactions to understand what is the old you versus the desired new you, to understand the why of your behaviors, and to begin to practice new behaviors. In Chapter Two I declared, "That which is not measured cannot be improved upon." This also applies to you.

Observing, watching, and monitoring you is effectively measuring you. Not with judgment but with compassion and a pure desire to understand why you are doing what you are doing and why you are not doing what you want to be doing.

In his book *The Happiness Trap*, author Russ Harris explains,

> "... there are two parts to the mind: the thinking Self—i.e., the part that is always thinking; the part that is responsible for all your thoughts, beliefs, memories, judgments, fantasies, etc. And then there's the observing Self—the part of your mind that is able to be aware of whatever you are thinking or feeling or doing at any moment. Without it, you couldn't develop those mindfulness skills. And the more you practice those mindfulness skills, the more you'll become aware of this part of your mind, and able to access it when you need it."[32]

Getting good at observing Self, like loving Self, takes time. It is a learned skill that is made easier by slowing down your actions and interactions, giving yourself space to contemplate, and particularly working at listening to your Self and the other person without distraction of thought. Just try it. In your next conversation with a loved one, try to be both in and outside the conversation. My wife Kate and I work at this a lot. And we are by no means perfect at it. We talk to express our needs, wants, and desires. And as we do, we observe how we are both verbalizing, listening, and responding to see if the exchange is founded on love or fear. And then on occasion we dissect what happened, including when one of us threw something on the floor ... this stuff is hard. So, the next time you have an opportunity for a serious chat with a loved one, try to listen without distraction, to suppress the fears of your Shadow Child, to feel compassion for the other person, and to accept all that he or she has to say without judgment. I guarantee that it won't be easy. I also guarantee that you and your loved one will walk away from that conversation in a better place than you would have.

Talk.

The journey to Self-Love, like the journey to a better life, is chock-full of land mines and sinkholes. And as much as it's a journey of the individual, it's a journey you should never undertake alone. We'll explore this more in the next chapter and Lesson #5, but for now, consider this: Learning to love you without condition requires putting all the crud—past, present, and future—on the table with someone. The presence of another, whether he or she is a therapist, psychic, or shaman, is a critical means to elevating the importance of your thoughts and feelings while providing feedback and perspective that helps you validate and invalidate your notions. Talking with a professional guide is, in a way, intimacy on training wheels. It's your chance to begin to learn how to extract the dark and the light from your heart and your head and share them with another without fear. Oh, and it is unbelievably cathartic.

My first conversation was with a psychic named Alex. It cost forty-five dollars for a half hour. I went to him not to understand my future, or even my past, but to understand me. And he told me three very helpful things:

1. My biggest struggle was that I was an artist in an engineer's body (Amen).
2. I had not yet learned how to feel.
3. I was sent here from another planet to learn emotion.

Okay, I know the third one is wacko. Although Kate might disagree.

The Alex conversation was like a door being cracked open, with a tiny stream of light coming through. And it served as my impetus to want to open it more. From there I started working with a string of psychotherapists, more psychics, and even mind-body healers. Each was profoundly helpful in very different ways. Each gave me the license to tell the truth about every part of my being, and in doing so, to learn how to forgive, accept, and embrace my whole.

In an article for *The Washington Post* by Michael O'Sullivan, Noah Baumbach, an American independent filmmaker, shared, "Part of therapy is being able to acknowledge the darker aspects of yourself.... Anybody who's had any therapy kind of discovers fairly quickly that there's a gap between your real self and the self you present to the world, no matter how self-actualized you are."[33]

Self-Love is about closing that gap. And therapy can really help. Sadly, only a tiny percentage of Americans take advantage of the field. While many claim issues of access and cost, and others declare it's only for those with serious mental illnesses, I think the real reason they don't seek psychotherapy is fear. The Shadow Child does not want to be found out.

So, once again you have a choice. Just as you must choose to evolve (innovate), choose to establish your point, and choose to make and follow your map, you must choose to talk about it all. So talk. And start by talking to your Shadow Child. If there is one conversation to have in all this, it is this: Tell your Shadow Child that you love him or her, that you understand him or her, and that you will take care of him or her. And then tell your child that you are in charge. That your Self is not him or her, and that he or she is not you. And then tell your child to go take a nap.

Write.

While talking is cathartic and contributory to your under-standing of you, writing can be too. As I've shared, docu-mentation is commitment, and it is an important confirmation that your thoughts and feelings are real. There can be periods of this journey to Self-Love where it all feels jumbled, where you start questioning the integrity of your thinking, and even why you are attempting what you are attempting. Writing makes it tangible; it allows you to sort things out and feels really good because you are letting it out.

Many people keep a journal, practicing the daily ritual of writing about topics or specific questions, including dream capture and interpretation. Others follow an idea proffered by Mark Bryan, Julia Cameron, and Catherine Allen, the authors of *The Artist's Way at Work*. They propose something called the Radio Kit, "initial bedrock tools (that) concern communication of Self to the Self."[34] The primary tool in the Kit is "the morning pages"—three longhand pages composed every morning that contain everything: "the flotsam and jetsam of your relation-ships; your concerns about your aging parents' health; your anger at the guy who took credit for your work in yesterday's meeting."[35] The idea is a regular, nonjudgmental, spontaneous capture of everything you feel and think. And in your unfiltered expression, you start to embrace the full truth of you and take a step toward Self-Love.

In my writing case, I chose poetry, in part because I love words, but also because I like the challenge of balancing the free flow of feeling with the creative desire to adhere to a particular rhyming structure. Over the course of my multi-year journey to Self-Love, I wrote scores of poems. Some were written for specific people, some to my Self, and many were written about or to Jarod, my Shadow Child. The poems found their way with little premeditation and tended to appear when I needed to either get something out or ponder something within. I learned how to write about Jarrod and to write to him in ways that allowed me to lessen his voice while finding my own. One example is this poem that I wrote for him way back when, not so coincidentally entitled "Fear."

Fear

Darkness descends
Pulling at my soul
Fear arises
Disabling my whole

The worry, the doubt
Eats away at my heart
The feeling of lessness
Rips me apart

The little boy inside
Wondering who will care
Burying his feelings
Unwilling to share

The hunger for comfort
The thirst for life
The need for companionship
A friend or a wife

Someone to trust
Who will not leave or deny
Who will hold my hand
As I reach for the sky

It is fear of not
Of not having love
Of not being cared for
By below or above

It is fear of rejection
Of being left by the road
People passing by
Living by a different code

Aloneness is the state
That creates the fear
But it is the mode
That I hold so dear

The contradiction is palpable
The truth quite profound
That what I fear most
Is my truth to be found

Whether good poems or bad, writing to Jarod and about Jarod made our separation clearer. He was not me, and I was not him. Over time I learned to love him as a part of me, but not have him be me. You have a Shadow Child. Start by naming him or her as a way of creating a dividing line. Don't overthink the name. I chose Jarod because it was the first name that appeared in my mind and because it felt like an older name, a name from my past, not my future. So, name your child, and then hug him or her and tell your child it's time for that nap. And when he or she gets up, share your thoughts, share your words, and share your love.

Let go of your Ego.

It is no doubt the hardest part. To let go of all the thoughts that riddle the mind, to let go of the neediness and the addiction to things. To let go of comparison, validation, and the constant quest to prove that we are worthy and lovable. It becomes a bit of a paradox. In order to achieve Self-Love, you must let go of your Ego and all that it carries. And yet in order to let go of your Ego, you must love your Self. So, what to do?

Imagine two straight lines, an "X," one heading up at a diagonal (your love of Self) and one heading down at a diagonal (the thirst of your Ego). In the beginning, the Self-Love part will be a distant shore and the Ego part will be dominating the conversation. Over time, through hard work, observation, talking, writing, and working at all this, the lines will eventually cross, and the Self part will edge upward, as Ego slips away. One day you will wake up and realize that the context of you has fundamentally shifted, and that incessant need has been replaced by unconditional Self-Love and the infinite capacity for intimacy. Quite amazing, really. But there's a slight hitch.

Self-Love is not a permanent state.

So, it turns out that even after all this work, all this letting go, all this observation, and migration to your true and lovable Self, once you get there, you are going to stumble every now and then. It turns out that the journey is a bit of a "two steps forward, one step back" type of affair. It turns out that Ego, like the Shadow Child, cannot be sent to bed forever. Every now and then he or she gets up, pops up, and throws us for a loop and at times causes a setback. Each and every day I am aware of Jarod, and there are days he is really, really needy. Days where I succumb to his fears and hold back on what I, Chris, really want to do.

But it's okay. As you have learned to embrace the dark and the light of Self, you learn to embrace the setbacks. As you have become observant of Self, you are aware of Ego's occasional intrusion and you handle it with aplomb. You say hello, you show compassion, and over time, not weeks but days or less, you send it away. Why? Because you love you.

Self-Love: the essential accelerant.

Sure, it's an accelerant, helping you apply the other six lessons more effectively and getting to your point faster. But it's also not really an option. The only way to really understand where you want to get to and how you want to get there (and with whom) is through loving Self. In loving Self you find the strength to make the sacrifices and take the risks to follow your map and achieve your point, while perhaps walking away from people and aspects of your past that simply do not honor you. In loving Self, you are able to let go of fear, need, and worry and instead focus on intimacy and realizing your truth, your Passions, and your Unique Capacities. Self-Love enables us to rise above the morass of our lives, to set our sights on a new way of being, and to be that way. It's hard as hell to do, but if you're still with me, you're halfway there.

Three Things You Should Do Now

1. Name your Shadow Child. Spend some quiet time contemplating him or her, his or her needs, and how his or her voice has been a part of your life and perhaps been confused with your own voice. And then decide what you'll call him or her. You'll be together forever, so you might as well be on a first-name basis.

2. Read some Maslow. Or at a minimum check out some of the videos about him. The more you understand the hierarchy of needs, the more you'll understand the journey to Self-Love.

3. Write down three things you love about your Self. I know this sounds absurdly simple. But you're hesitating anyway, right? Proves my point. Now do it. Or better yet, write your Self a poem. Rhyming not required.

there are only two tribes

I'm glad you and your Shadow Child are still with me. If you've been observing your Self while you've been reading, you've probably had thoughts and feelings ranging from moments of confusion and tiny little epiphanies to random chuckles sprinkled with intermittent doubt about me, about you, about the whole topic of innovating your life. And unless you're a member of one of the *This Is It* Reading Clubs that are sprouting up all over the world (insert smirking face) you have probably also felt pangs of loneliness. Like it's completely up to you to do all this stuff. Particularly the Self-Love part.

Well, it's not. In fact, the completely ironic thing about self-help is that you can't really do it alone. And the same is true of entrepreneurship. Solo entrepreneurs rarely make it. Even with the best map in the world, the only way you can get from where you are to the point you want to be is with the help of other people. And I'm talking about more than you, your Shadow Child, and a capable shrink. People need people to innovate.

So, as much as I believe in the importance of consulting the professionals, the therapists, the shaman, and the witch doctors,

I also believe in the essential task of surrounding yourself with a lot of other kinds of people.

As Parker Palmer writes in his seminal book *A Hidden Wholeness—The Journey Toward an Undivided Life*:

> "The journey toward inner truth is too taxing to be made solo: lacking support, the solitary traveler soon becomes weary or fearful and is likely to quit the road.

> "The path is too deeply hidden to be traveled without company: finding our ways involves clues that are subtle and sometimes misleading, requiring the kind of discernment that can happen only in dialogue.

> "The destination is too daunting to be achieved alone: we need community to find the courage to venture into the alien lands to which the inner teacher may call us."[36]

Right on. We need dialogue, we need community, and we need peeps, but not just any peeps. We need the people who embrace our quest as their own and exist in part to help us and others complete it. And it turns out that the roughly 7.5 billion people on the planet right now pretty much divide into two camps: the ones who get it and the ones who don't.

Which brings us to *This Is It* Lesson #5: *There Are Only Two Tribes. At its simplest, the world is made up of seekers and non-seekers. And to realize your point, you need to surround your Self with seekers. You need to connect with your Tribe.*

The nature of your existence depends on other people's natures.

Finding the seekers, finding your Tribe, is fundamentally about searching for truth, a concept perfectly captured by Jeffrey Masson, the prolific author of several books focused on the emotional life of animals. Yep, animals. In his bestselling book, *Dogs Never Lie About Love,* he shares, "Questers of the truth, that's who dogs are; seekers after the invisible scent of another being's authentic core."[37]

I love this even though the visual of butt sniffing comes to mind. You and I are dogs in search of our authentic core and the core of others. Woof. And know that all your sniffing will no doubt result in finding the authentic ones, which will have a huge impact on how you want to be and your ability to reach your point. In Chapter Two we explored how to determine your point, and I presented this seemingly simple (but not really) equation:

Your Point = Passion (Why of you) + Unique Capacities (What of you) x Desired Nature of Existence (How you want to be)

I also explained that the Desired Nature of Existence variable was both the murkiest and the most important. Damn it. It is a force multiplier versus an additive because the tone of our lives has such a huge impact on how we feel about our lives. Our environment, the people in it, the energy we experience, and the love we realize (or don't) are the greatest contributors to both our ability to see our point and to achieve it. The Nature of our Existence informs everything. It's oxygen. Without it, we might as well pull the plug.

It serves as a declaration of the kind of life you want to live as measured by the interactions within it. And that means interactions primarily with other people (unless you want to include domesticated animals, which is totally fine by me). I wrote "The Nature of our Existence is the lubricant for us realizing our Passion and unlocking the full power of our Unique Capacities." Who we interact with, how we interact with them, what we exchange, and what we feel between us are the most critical facets of our lives. Why, you ask? Because we are human. We are social animals. It's true whether you're an introvert or an extrovert or something in-between. Surrounding your Self with members of the right Tribe will pretty much guarantee that the Nature of Your Existence is the way you want it to be. Let me show you what I mean.

Take a moment to think and feel about your life right now and how people around you impact the inside of you and the Nature of Your Existence. If you're game, take out a large piece of white paper and your now blunted and bloodied black Sharpie and write down the first names of ten people from work, at home, or in your life who affect how your life feels. These are people that are on your heart radar regularly, who cross your mind more than once a day—people that you associate with some meaningful emotion. Next to each person's name simply indicate two things: a plus or a minus, and a short phrase, complimentary or not, that you link with that person. It's okay to be a little snarky here (as long as my name's not on the list). Here's my version of this exercise (the names have been changed to avoid pissing anyone off):

Anne	+	Keeps me thinking
Jane	–	Painfully inconsistent
Ellen	–	Incapable of real sharing
Mark	+	Steady, positive force
Jim	+	Caring, challenge to pin down
Henry	+	Supportive, not fully open
Linda	+	Completely aligned, loving
John	–	Nothing to share, negative

| Melissa | + | Early but trying |
| Laura | + | Incredibly strong, clear |

(IM: What one person is absolutely in your Tribe? What one person is absolutely not?)

Revealing, eh? Hopefully you'll have more names with pluses than minuses, but more importantly you will see and sense just how important the people around you are in terms of determining both how you feel about today and about your ability to get to where you want to go tomorrow. The irony of this list is that these people are not material things, and yet they are the most material aspect of your life, right? Some of them are fuel; some of them are foe. Some are central to your Desired Nature of Existence, and some should clearly not be in the picture. Who they are and how they are with you, what they do for you, and what they don't do for you really matter. Which makes the "management" of this list an essential task in your efforts to get to your point, to get to a better life. The goal over time is to have the ten names all be positive contributors to your daily life, and to be able to spot and remove the negative folks as soon as they appear.

What your Tribe does for you, exactly.

Your Tribe walks the Earth to learn, to see, to understand, to get to their own points, and as importantly, to help you realize yours. They are all at different stages on the journey—some just starting out, some nearing the end (if there were an end). They are working on all the same stuff: letting go of Ego, loving Self, pushing away fear, and seeking unconditional love for their Selves and for all others. They are attempting to follow a similar lesson book, probably obtained from one of those Chopra or Covey characters.

I know, I know, this sounds like some sort of Buddha-Angel-Missionary mash-up. It's not. They're not. They are just people like you and me who are simply trying to get to a better place. They are not here to solve your problems or fix you, but rather to allow you to realize your truth without fear, shame, or discomfort. They are here to remind you that all this is right, the dark and the light, and to reassure you that you are not alone in this quest. They are here as examples of both how easy and how hard this journey can be. They are here to show you love without requite and understanding without resolution, to provide a gentle embrace and a reminder that it's all good, it's all okay. Listen, as I've stated ad nauseum, this journey is really hard. Your Tribe exists not to make it easier but to provide the support and succor to help you keep trudging in the trenches. And that's why you are here for them.

I'm guessing that way back when, this was partly why religious communities formed. To provide a gentle reminder that there is a path, that it is worth taking, and that we are not alone. Our collective humanity is what defines us. Remember my reference in the Introduction to the most common regret of dying people? The biggest, most consistent regret is the lack of relationships, the lack of embracing other people—the lack of spending time with members of the right Tribe.

The signs of the right Tribe.

So, if there are only two Tribes, how can you tell the difference? And what exactly are you looking for? What are the signals and signs that someone is a member of the right Tribe? First, let's blow up any notion that this is about pedigree, ethnicity, age, or any of the other bias-laden markers we use to delineate who we might be comfortable with. Your Tribe knows no geographic boundary, no demographic filter, and no socioeconomic strata. Its members are of every age, every religion, and every background. What they have in common is this: They are committed to their personal evolution and the evolution of others.

This is *not* about finding people we "click with." It's about finding people who honor and support us in our life journey and our effort to realize Self and our Big Hairy Audacious Point (remember that?). And the good news is that they are everywhere, representing every nook and cranny of life. They are the guy at the gas station, the neighbor two doors down, and the co-worker who says good morning every morning. They are close friends from school (but not all of them) and complete strangers who oddly enough can feel more connected to us than members of our own family (more on this later).

To find your Tribe, there's a bit of a Catch-22 you have to work through, harkening back to Lesson #4 and the concept of Self-Love. To achieve Self-Love, you need the help of your Tribe, and to find your Tribe, you need to be on the road to finding Self-Love.

Twenty years ago, when my Ego ruled and my love of Self was in the toilet, I couldn't find a thing, including my Tribe. As I began to find my way to Self-Love and to intimacy, all of a sudden people began appearing to help me. Melissa, the long-lost friend from college who became my daily guide for the first couple of years. Marc and Danielle, the couple who moved in downstairs and who showed me the power of love through their example. Rob, a guy who gave up his company to work by my side. People from the past, people from the present, all accidentally but really contributed mightily to my future. It's quite amazing that way.

So, the good news is that the Catch-22 is not really a catch. All this stuff is a do-able migration away from one state toward another, a shift of our equilibrium, a shift of emphasis. If I can do this, so can you.

To help you along, here is a cheat sheet on the sure signs someone is a member of your Tribe. And remember, everyone is on a spectrum on this stuff; nobody is perfect. We're all actively working on being more of these things, and in some cases, we might have even slipped backward. That is completely okay and completely normal. What's important is that we all embrace the traits and are working at fully realizing them.

Use the following list as a checklist to determine whether someone in your midst could be a member of your seeker Tribe. More than five checks usually mean it's pretty damn likely that person is in your Tribe or on his or her way to joining. Hug that person quickly. Consider letting the others go.

The Seven Traits of Tribespeople

#1: Honesty. Members of the Tribe work at being unapologetically honest. Candor is their universal way as long as it hurts no one. They never hesitate to share every element on their Balance Sheet, the good, the bad, and the ugly. And they have no shame or sadness about it. When I get "accused" of being too candid, more often than not the accuser is not a member of my Tribe. The only time we/they check their honesty is when the sharing is meant to hurt. Not cool.

#2: Open. Their arms, brains, hearts, and souls are wide, wide open. They are open to all, emotionally, intellectually, and spiritually. They have little fear of what might be on the other side, believing that connection with everything and everybody is central to the route they are following on their map.

#3: Curious. They have an unquenchable thirst for learning about pretty much anything. They read, they ponder, they ask. They are truly, unabashedly seekers. All content is worth consuming, and social media is not the mother lode. They want to understand the meaning of things and constantly enrich their perspectives and capacities to engage with the world.

#4: Nonjudgmental. They carry few biases and work hard to eliminate the stragglers. They see all in the world as worthy, including the other Tribe, the non-seekers.

#5: Compassion. They are kind, considerate, and loving. They genuinely care for all others and have a remarkable ability to forgive. (I am not so good at the forgiving part, but hey, I'm trying!)

#6: Peaceful. They are not at war. They are content to move forward, often at a snail's pace, believing that the measure is progress, not conquest. They come in peace, they live in peace, and they leave in peace. They are really good at not taking the bait. (I am also not so great at this.)

#7: Self-Love. It's clear that they're doing pretty well pushing Ego away and embracing Intimacy in its stead, including their capacity to be intimate with you. But remember, they are on the journey too. They aren't done yet, and in the spirit of the #1 trait, *Honesty*, most likely never will be.

Okay, so anybody coming to mind? If you want to work through this a bit more, take your list of ten people and contemplate each relationship against the checklist. And don't freak out if you don't end up with a ton of tribespeople. Twenty years ago, my list was not very long. And yet today many members of the right Tribe surround me, people from every walk of life, of every age, of every everything, engaging with me in ever-growing concentric circles.

You will need to go around in circles to get to your point.

I've been hung up on circles ever since I was a kid. Remember Leonardo da Vinci and the anatomical drawing of a man, arms and legs extended to capture our proportions as a circle? Since the beginning of time, circles have been held up as the perfect form, from Yin and Yang to the dudes in armor sitting at the Round Table. Circles reflect balance, equality, infinity, and more. We are designed as a circle, life is a circle, and we need circles around us to realize our Self and our point. And oh, by the way, the swing and throw of any kind in any sport is a perfect circle. Which is why I suck at golf.

Bestselling author Madisyn Taylor shares on her website, DailyOM, that ". . . people who take part in a circle find that their power increases exponentially while with the group. Like a drop of water rippling on the surface of a pond, the waves of energy produced in a circle radiate outward in circular motion. While one person may act like a single beacon that emanates light, a circle of people is like a satellite dish that sends out energy. There is power in numbers, and when the commitment is made by many to face one another, clasp hands, and focus on one intention, their circle emanates ripples of energy that can change the world."[38]

Your Tribe is effectively a series of concentric circles, beginning with you and your family. Start harnessing their power.

The circles of you and your family.

The innermost circle really is you. It's small in circumference but mighty in impact. Not the anatomical you, but the Self-Loving you. This circle represents the infinite dance between Self and Ego, the push and the pull, the ever-shifting attempt by your Shadow Child to dominate the conversation. It's a circle because it goes around and around. The journey to Self-Love never ends. So, you might as well get going.

The next circle out is the circle of you and your birth family, specifically your parents and siblings. In theory this should be your core Tribe, right? The tribe of tribes, the family sanctum, the people who get you and this journey you're on better than anyone. After all, you are connected by DNA and RNA, which means you are connected in the most intimate way possible.

Umm, not always. Actually, not often. While I firmly believe much in life is a choice (see Lesson #7), your birth family is not. And just because you are from the same gene pool does not mean you are on the same page.

In fact, according to author Terence T. Gorski in his book *Getting Love Right*, 70 to 80 percent of Americans come from dysfunctional families. He writes,

> "To say that a family is dysfunctional is to say that it *doesn't work*: It doesn't provide to a minimum degree what its members need for mental, physical, and emotional well-being. By contrast, a functional family is one that teaches children how to think clearly and act responsibly, to understand their feelings, and relate to others in a healthy way. It equips them with the mental, emotional, and living skills to deal with life as an adult. To the extent that your family failed to teach you these important skills, it was dysfunctional."[39]

Whoops. My birth family gets the big C, or at least a B–. Which is not to say we do not love each other, but it is to say that most of our members would not get five or more checks on the tribal trait checklist. How about yours?

So, what do you do if your birth family is not part of your Tribe and cannot be one of your innermost circles of support? The first thing to do is to suck it up and accept it. Just like you accept the good, the bad, and the ugly of you, it's critical that you accept the same of them. They are just members of the other Tribe. They are not less than, nor are they pagans. They simply speak a different language and look at the world and their lives through a different lens. Remember Tribespeople Trait #4: You're working to be nonjudgmental.

The second thing to do is work on changing how you communicate with them, not with the expectation that your words will change them but rather because it is an act of honoring your Self. As a member of the Tribe, Trait #1 is honesty. In my own journey, the acts of sharing my separation and ultimate divorce, my commitment to therapy, my decision to quit drinking, and all the other changes I made were met by my family with either no response or an incredulous "What in god's name for?" Ouch. Not helpful, somewhat hurtful. But necessary. Again, the intent of sharing was not to change them but rather to be true to me. Bearing our truth is an act of Self-Love. It is cathartic to declare without shame and to speak with conviction. When you speak from the heart, your soul is aligned, and that serves as motivation to keep innovating along the path to your point, to a better life.

Interestingly, over the last twenty years I have seen glimmers of change, glimmers of an emerging understanding by some of my family members that my life of intimacy guided by intention and my language of the heart may actually be the better way to go. And that recognition has in a way brought us closer together.

If you are a parent, the third thing to do with this assessment is to decide to stop perpetuating the crappy grade of your birth family with your own children. We parent as we were parented. So, if you do not want to end up as a dysfunctional family, start by declaring a different point. Remember the point of parenting? If you want your children or nieces and nephews to view their birth family as an essential, supportive circle and core part of their Tribe, then be intentional about creating one. You can use the Tribal Trait checklist as a guide for what you're after or read Dr. Elvira Aletta's work on the topic in her blog "Explore What's Next." She's a PhD and therapist who spends a ton of her time contemplating the question of what informs a functional family. And she's identified seventeen attributes. It's a long list, so here are my top three picks, in her words from her website:

R-E-S-P-E-C-T

"Respect is the Holy Grail of functional families. All people in the family, brothers to sisters, mothers to fathers, parents to kids must be respectful as consistently as possible. Being considerate of each other is the tie that binds, even more than love. I think too much emphasis is put on love in general. I've heard of many atrocities done within families in the name of love but never in the name of respect. Just about all the things on the list come out of respect first."

An emotionally safe environment . . .

"All members of the family can state their opinions, thoughts, wants, dreams, desires, and feelings without fear of being slammed, shamed, belittled, or dismissed."

. . . allows people to change and grow.

"It used to be people in the family were labeled the smart one or the pretty one, the funny one or the shy one. While that's not done so overtly anymore, labeling is still something to watch. A functional family lets people define themselves. Individual differences are appreciated, even celebrated. It also lets the kids become independent when it's appropriate and come back to the safety of the family when they need nurturing. The adults in the family need to be allowed to grow as well. A mother may want to get a graduate degree, or a father may decide to retire early and start something new. These changes merit discussion on how they will affect everyone in the family, adjustment, perhaps negotiation, but again, if done with respect everyone can be satisfied."[40]

(IM: Think about your birth family and these three criteria. Be honest.)

Not to confuse you, but you can start to see some overlap here between Dr. Aletta's call for respect, emotional safety, and opportunity for growth; the seven traits; and the seven *This Is It* lessons. Whether the desired outcome is a better life, a better relationship, or a better family, the same basic principles are at work. The real question isn't what they are; the real question is whether you are willing to apply them. And nowhere is that truer than when it comes to your significant other.

The circle of the significant other (or BFF).

Okay, here we go, the third circle out, the one between you and your significant other or, lacking one of those, how about your BFF? In theory, this circle should be made of titanium and steel, impenetrable to the enemy and able to withstand onslaughts of psychic calamity and occasional emotional drought. Well, according to the latest divorce statistics, not so much. In order for this circle to be part of your Tribe, you will naturally want your SO/BFF to embody all seven traits of Tribespeople. The rub is that the odds are against that happening. The odds are that the love of your life or Best Friend Forever is not quite where you want him or her to be. Do it. Go down the checklist. My guess is that you're not checking every box, right? And you're beginning to feel a little queasy.

The stark reality is a bit much. It's okay. Breathe in, breathe out. Half the battle is acknowledging what's really going on. The other half is deciding to do something about it. And the good news is that you don't need to make him or her the paradigm of tribal purity or jump ship and call the divorce lawyer stat. What you need, the Minimum Viable Product (Partner) in startup parlance, is for your sig or BFF to be open to his or her own evolution and respectful of you and your journey. Absent that, I fear for your partnership.

Sorry, but it's true. Alignment around intention, around a desire to get to a different point, is critical. Because the biggest source of friction between unhappy couples is that one wants to grow and the other does not.

Assuming you've checked a couple of boxes and believe that your partner or pal is sort of on board with the journey, the next task is to pick courage over fear and begin the conversations with him or her that will hopefully forge and strengthen your circle. I know the bile is rising. But remember, it is not taking on our fears that kills most partnerships. It certainly killed mine. It is the fear-induced inability to say what we feel, to ask for what we want, to share our truth, and to hold the other person accountable for their part of the deal.

I'm not going to belabor the importance of this circle or of you taking action to make it stronger, to bring it toward the center of your Tribe. It's your choice. Lesson #7 again. And it may be the most important choice you ever make. Sorry for the drama.

Parker Palmer's Circles of Trust.

I love Parker Palmer's writings. And I particularly love his concept of Circles of Trust that he explores in *A Hidden Wholeness*. Circles of Trust are the next concentric ring out in the formation of your Tribe. According to Parker, Circles of Trust "combine unconditional love, or regard, with hopeful expectancy, creating a space that both safeguards and en-courages the inner journey. In such a space, we are freed to hear our own truth, touch what brings us joy, become self-critical about our faults, and take risky steps toward change—knowing that we will be accepted no matter the outcome."[41] Circles of Trust are 100 percent nonjudgmental, 100 percent *not* about solving your problem, and 100 percent about each participant as an individual within a community.

They are about learning to be, to share, to explore, to be honored, and most importantly, to not fear the truth of our Self and our intentions.

I really love this line from his book:

> "A Circle of Trust consists of relationships that are neither invasive nor evasive."[42]

Contrast that statement with most relationships. Invasive as in the other person or people relentlessly pushing us, subjecting us to their biases, even solving our problem for us when we have not asked them to solve our problem. Evasive as in the other person is holding back, not willing to share his or her truth or to ask the difficult questions that will reveal the difficult answer that everyone knows, but no one is brave enough to say.

Sound familiar? What this definition sets up is how many of our relationships are not actually circles of trust. They are circles of convenience, of familiarity, even of friendship. But they are not circles of unconditional trust. It's time to start correcting that. It's time to start building and maybe even rebuilding circles of trust. To look at all the friends around us and determine first who are the seekers and who are not, and then to begin to build specific circles of trust that provide us with the support and motivation we need to stay on the path that leads to our point. And if you want the specific Circle of Trust how-tos, read Parker's book.

The Circle of Strangers.

The last circle in your quest to find your Tribe is the Circle of Strangers. And oddly enough, strangely enough, it is the easiest circle to build. It's easy because unlike with our significant others and family members, there is little risk. We don't fear losing people we don't know. After all, they're strangers! It's easy because we don't fear not being accepted by them. After all, who the hell are they? And it's easy because there are a lot of them; they're all around us each and every day. But remember, there are two Tribes. Not all strangers are part of the right Tribe, your Tribe. So, the question is how to identify your Tribespeople in a crowd.

The simplest way is to exhibit the traits of the Tribespeople, and you will readily see or not see those traits in everyone you meet. It's akin to speaking a foreign language. If you speak it, only those who understand and speak it too will be able to respond. Over time, as you become more and more fluent in the language, your capacity to quickly identify fellow Tribespeople will also increase. And at some point, you'll be able to walk into any situation, from a cocktail party full of acquaintances to a gaggle of commuters waiting at a bus stop, and immediately determine who is part of your Tribe.

Years ago, early in my work, a friend suggested I connect with a guy named Joe Knowles, ostensibly about business stuff. I reached out, and we agreed to have a coffee at the Harvard School of Public Health where Joe was getting his Master's. We met at 2 p.m. I walked out four hours later. An hour "business conversation" had become a freewheeling, open kimono connection that has only gotten more intense and intimate over the last ten years.

Oddly enough, of all the circles in your Tribe, this is the one that at times provides the most motivation to keep going. While the circles of Self, of your birth family, of your significant other, and of Trust can carry more real power, it's the Circle of Strangers that can serve as the most consistent reminder that you are not alone and that this journey is good.

In an article for *The Christian Science Monitor*, journalist Bill Moyer said it well: "Our very lives depend on the ethics of strangers, and most of us are always strangers to other people."[43]

The Circle of Strangers has become a huge source of motivation and happiness for me. As I explained to someone recently, when you walk the Earth with your arms wide open, free to share, to be intimate, and to show your true Self, the simplest, most innocuous of conversations can become quite remarkable. Within minutes and sometimes seconds, people you do not know at all become a part of your life, a part of your journey, and significant contributors to the Nature of your Existence. Strangers become intimate friends, even if you will never see them again. Mundane acts become almost magical moments that re-affirm why you're working so hard at all this and remind you of how much progress you have made. And the more you engage this way, the more people and opportunities will cross your path to further encourage you and help you get to your point.

It's called the Law of Attraction. And it works.

Beware the energy suckers, naysayers, and charlatans.

I forgot to mention something. These people exist: people who may appear to be part of your Tribe but are actually not. As you begin to build and strengthen your circles, and as you engage strangers while exhibiting the traits and speaking the language of the Tribespeople, you will no doubt come across energy suckers, naysayers, and charlatans. They are not just members of the other Tribe, they are negative forces that you need to walk away from, and quickly.

The energy suckers tend to be people who may feign tribal traits, but in actuality are so far away from Self-Love that they are desperately, even if subconsciously, trying to suck the love and energy out of others. Including you. I know you know whom I mean. They are takers, not givers. And you can't afford them. Staying on your path is hard enough, and you'll need every ounce of emotional and spiritual energy to keep going. Giving up your energy for nothing in return is both costly and disrespectful of you.

Naysayers are the second sect of the other Tribe that is really dangerous and a must to avoid. They can exist within every circle, including and often particularly in your birth family. They will never read this book. They don't embrace evolution of Self, the concept of Self-Love, intimacy—none of it. At their core, they are stuck in Ego and even more paralyzed than we are or have been. They live in abject fear of change, of exposure, and use denial as a shield. They will ridicule your words, challenge your intentions, and worse. If you go back to the ten people exercise, my bet is some of those names listed are naysayers. Don't try to convert them. Just hug them and choose to spend less of your time with them.

And the third group, perhaps the most insidious and difficult to discern group, is the charlatans. They talk the talk but never really walk the walk. They drank the Kool-Aid but spat it out when no one was looking. They will appear to be supportive and ready to join your Circle of Trust, but they are not sincere; they are not clear on what this is really all about. They may not even know they are charlatans. Their Ego is alive and well and their Shadow Child is pulling all the strings. Again, hug them and choose to spend less of your time with them.

Peace, love, and understanding.

The evolutionary journey to your point and a better life is difficult. It is confusing. And it is riddled with fear and doubt, with your Shadow Child doing a ton of backseat driving even though he or she has no license. It is a daily struggle to stay focused, to remember all that you have learned, and to keep motivated as you attempt to live by the seven *This Is It* lessons. The challenges are such that we need constant feeding, a steady flow of solace and support; we need peace, love, and understanding, the essential nutrients that can only, will only, come from your Tribe, from the seekers who are on the same path as you.

While there is much work to be done on many fronts, this tribal work is pretty straightforward. Start looking at the people in your life and determining which side of the tribal ledger they are on. And start working toward being more on the right side. Because you cannot do this alone. And doing it with others is an essential part of what it means to innovate your life.

Three Things You Should Do Now

1. Write out the Seven Traits of Tribespeople and start looking at the people around you through that lens. Judge the picture you see not as the end but as an opportunity to surround your Self with motivation and reward.

2. Share what you've learned thus far with your parent, significant other, or BFF. Tell them about your point and what you're trying to do. Your hands will be clammy, but it's a really important step.

3. Talk to strangers. And I mean talk. Start practicing the language. You'll either have a great conversation or no conversation at all. And that's to be expected. Because there are only two Tribes.

work and life are one

Thanks for sticking with me. Only two more lessons to go! Hopefully, you're now madly in love with your Self, you've dumped a bunch of one-dimensional friends, you're building fabulous Circles of Trust, and you can literally taste the promise of a better life: nectarine sweet with a hint of savory something, right? Um, maybe, but probably not. Because this stuff is damn hard. As I keep trying to tell you, there is no simple flicking of a switch to realize your point. The tasks are many, complicated, arduous, and can even be a little distasteful! Sucking up your fears, telling your Shadow Child to go outside and play, and getting to a place where you are looking in the mirror and smiling at what you see can be brutally difficult. Even the "Three Things You Can Do Now" exercises at the end of each chapter are kind of a pain in the ass. I get it. But if you don't try, what have you done? Reading this book becomes just another form of lip service—all talk, no walk. So, what say you start walking? I'll go with you.

And on the walk, understand that even with the best of maps and efforts, this is a decidedly up-one-hill-down-the-other journey, a journey that requires a load of resilience and the recognition that all the pieces of your life are part of the same puzzle. They must fit together just so in order for you to realize your point. And the puzzle necessarily consists of work and life components. Sure, people take on crappy jobs to make a living and then seek to live and realize their real desires outside of work. But the problem with that is how work has intruded on our lives. A separation is no longer an option for most of us. Which presents Lesson #6: *Work and Life Are One. In order to realize your point, to realize the full possibility of your life, it's imperative that you align what you do for a living with how you want to live.*

Allow me to provide a little more living color.

In the beginning, when most humans made their living by digging in the dirt, they effectively lived integrated lives. There was no separation between the thing called work and the thing called life. Back then you farmed to live and you lived to farm. And then it all changed with the arrival of something called a steam engine. Poof, work and life separated. Instead of plucking chickens for dinner, we started punching clocks. Suddenly work-life integration became work-life segregation. Dad went off to work every morning and came back at dusk. Mom stayed home and ironed. Weeknights were for watching *Father Knows Best*, and weekends were for mowing the lawn and building train sets with the kids. Choo, choo. Your job was your job, and your life was your life. There were clear lines of demarcation. You contentedly or not so contentedly put your head down and worked, and when you lifted it up, you went home. This, my friend, was the American dream.

And then it all changed again, with the big bang arrival of gigabits, terabytes, and this unnatural phenomenon called the World Wide Web. Having 24/7 access to everything turned into an undeclared, kinda crazy but very real expectation that workers be available 24/7, which began to erode the barriers between work and life. As the barriers crumbled, the dust kicked up, and work intrusion on life increased, there began a call (really more like a loud whisper) for individuals and companies to embrace "work-life balance." The segregated model was replaced by the never-ending quest to find equilibrium between the demands of work and the needs of life.

It turns out the balance quest is never-ending because it's downright impossible. Don Quixote and windmill stuff. The root problem with the concept of work-life balance and finding equilibrium is that it presumes you can maintain separation. And that just ain't so in today's world. It simply can't be done. It's poppycock.

Laura Vanderkam, the author of the book *I Know How She Does It: How Successful Women Make the Most of Their Time,*[44] did a longitudinal study of how high-earning female workers lived their lives. Of those studied, 75 percent did something personal during work-hours and 77 percent worked outside of work-hours. Work and life are no longer discrete propositions; they cannot be managed as separate events, which makes the whole idea of balance questionable and problematic. Balance implies a teeter-totter. When one side goes up, the other must come down. When one side is going in a good direction, the other must be going in a bad direction, or perhaps one side is getting more and the other side is getting less. Regardless of the context, a trade-off is happening. When you're being a great employee, you must be willing to be a not-so-great parent or spouse or even friend. I have to say that's a pretty depressing—and to my mind unacceptable—view of the way life has to be.

So, the concept of work-life balance is a fundamentally flawed pipe dream further fueled by the ugly reality of our 24/7, hyper-competitive, globally connected world, where many if not most companies and organizations are manically, desperately driving worker productivity in order not to thrive but just to survive. And that means the pressure they put on their workers is unrelenting and the expectations ever-growing. How many of us look at work emails over the weekend? (A survey conducted in 2013 by Opinion Matters, a market research firm, provided the answer: 81 percent. I bet it's gone way up since then. Crazy.) How many of us who have hourly-wage jobs are called into work off-schedule with virtually no notice? (Another survey conducted by the U.S. Bureau of Labor Statistics suggests anywhere from 30 to 50 percent.) How many of us effectively never stop working? (Ask your friends or look in the mirror. Or better yet, stop looking at your work emails on your smartwatch.)

So, if you can't maintain separation in order to achieve equilibrium, then what the hell do you do? Buying a one-way plane ticket to Costa Rica is an option. The other slightly more practical if less escapist choice is to go after *work-life integration*, to become a farmer of your life (back to the future, please) where your work feeds you and vice versa. Where everything you do at work and outside of work is a contributor to or manifestation of the way you want to live. It all becomes one big honker way of living that helps get you to your point.

And to help prove my point, how about another Steve Jobs quote, from his commencement address at Stanford in 2005:

> "Your work is going to fill a large part of your life, and the only way to be truly satisfied is to do what you believe is great work. And the only way to do great work is to love what you do. If you haven't found it yet, keep looking. Don't settle. As with all matters of the heart, you'll know when you find it."[45]

(But what about the garbage man, Steve? What about the single mom who has three kids, works two jobs, and struggles to put food on the table? Fair issue. My stuff is a decidedly and slightly ashamedly white-collar, privileged view for sure that sadly does not apply in full to every life. But I still aver that everyone could and should work harder to align their work with the life they want to live, even if that just means looking at who they surround themselves with at work. So, if you're picking up trash barrels every day, picking the right trash company to work for should make a difference, right?)

There is work-life integration, and there is work-life integration.

I need to be clear here. My view of work-life integration is totally different than what the rest of the world is talking about. The increasingly accepted definition in HR circles is based on the idea that technology now allows people to live and work interchangeably. In this quote from an article for *Fast Company,* Dean Douglas says it all:

> "In today's ever-updating, ever-mobile work-forces, a professional's time is precious, and he or she wants to optimize it as effectively as possible. Professionals in all industries are casting out the notions of work-life balance in order to build better work-life integration practices—where work and life are intertwined—by leveraging technology to make it happen."[46]

Dean, you're clearly a smart dude, but you make us sound like cold, calculating automatons. Geez. Sure, we can use technology to buy our kid a new pair of Nikes while we're on a video conference call with the office in Singapore. Sure, we can get it all done by using our new coola woola web app to toggle between life and work, between this task and that. But is that really a good thing? Does checking stuff off our work and life to-do lists make us happy? Does it get us any closer to our point?

Of course, it doesn't.

You know what does? Work-life integration that is focused not on real-time toggling between tasks but on having what you do for work be an enabler of and manifestation of your point. Remember the point equation?

Your Point = Passion (Why of you) + Unique Capacities (What of you) x Desired Nature of Existence (How you want to be)

Let's apply the equation variables to my recent gig as the managing director of the Harvard Innovation Labs:

My point: To help thousands, maybe even millions of people realize their full potential, their possibility.

I got to advise hundreds of students and alumni and speak to thousands on how to grow their startups and, in doing so, grow themselves. Check.

My passion: To help people, and specifically to apply creativity and clarity to their personal and professional challenges.

As the managing director, I got to do this not just with students and alumni but with the entire Harvard Innovation Labs staff. I was helping all of them realize their greatest possibilities. Check.

My unique capacities: My friends, employees, and clients tell me I am uniquely capable of helping them see and realize new possibilities by listening well, working hard to understand their realities, and then helping them craft a simple but effective path to a different place.

This is what I pretty much do on a day in and day out basis. I get paid for it. Check.

My desired nature of existence: To surround myself with honesty, intimacy of thought and heart, and creative seekers who want to engage in meaningful, compelling ways. Check, again.

The students, alumni, and staff involved with the Harvard Innovation Labs are first and foremost seekers. Open to everything, honest about everything, and looking to understand what is and what could be in the deepest of ways.

So, I'm lucky, or perhaps just really intentional. I am farming my life by doing work that nurtures me, fulfills me, and takes advantage of the full me. My work and life are one. As Bill Burnett, the Stanford director of design and the co-author of the must-read book *Designing Your Life* declares:

> "A coherent life is one lived in such a way that you can clearly connect the dots between three things: who you are, what you believe, what you are doing."[47]

Or in slightly simpler vernacular, what you do for a living should be aligned with how you want to live. Period.

(IM: How aligned is your life right now?)

The feeling is more important than the function.

If work feels good and feels aligned with what you want to be doing and how you want to live, work is no longer work. Well, sure it's still work, but it's not work the way we tend to think about work: drudgery and necessity versus elation and opportunity. Stephen Cope, the renowned psychotherapist and director of the Kripalu Institute for Extraordinary Living, captured the idea in his recent book *The Great Work of Your Life*:

> "We work first because we have to work. Then because we want to work. Then because we love to work. Then

the work simply does us. Difficult at the beginning. Inevitable at the end."[48]

I'm not sure about the inevitable part. I am sure of the following: Work that is not work is love, and love that is not love is work.

To ensure the chances of our work being love, I suggest we not rely on that possibility and instead make some more intentional choices to ensure that it happens—which reminds me of a recent conversation with a pal of mine, Daniel. He laid out his career path scenario in this binary choice way: Go after the money or go after a lower-paying job that offered more flexibility. I proposed that there was another way of thinking about it. Instead of focusing on the function, focus on the feeling. Specifically, how did he want to feel in his day-to-day life and what kind of role and environment would enable that? It's an exercise I did years ago, when I had an incredibly cushy job that I increasingly hated. I began to ask my Self the Passion, Unique Capacities, and Desired Nature of Existence questions. And it helped me see that I wanted a role and a life that allowed me to lead, that provided open-ended creative opportunity, and that took full advantage of my communication abilities with people at work and people at play. So, I quit. And started my own creative agency. And moved to Boston from the 'burbs. And the rest, as they say, is history. God, what a silly expression.

The feeling versus function thing is also the core of the advice I dispensed at Harvard to newly minted or about to be graduates beginning the job search. Instead of trying to find a job, try to find an environment that will move you, nurture you, and help connect you with you. The functional stuff will take care of itself.

I am living proof. My first real job out of college was as a desk clerk at a hotel in Washington, D.C. The function was irrelevant.

I checked guests in; I checked guests out. Mundane stuff. What mattered was that the company was progressive, open-minded, innovative, thoughtful, and caring—attributes that very much aligned with who I was or at least wanted to be. Subsequently, three years after signing on as a desk clerk I was promoted to vice president of advertising and national sales for the entire chain. I was twenty-five years old.

Nuts, right? Well, not really. Because I was in an environment that aligned with who I was, an environment that valued the way of me and rewarded it, I wanted to give the company all I had. And in giving all I had, I kept getting more and more responsibility and opportunity. That episode and virtually every career move I've made since has resulted in this basic belief: The functional stuff (and the material gain) will come if the feeling is right.

Trust me. Actually, don't trust me. Give it a whirl.

And do the math.

Okay, so if I haven't convinced you with my compelling storytelling, let's try a more quantitative approach. My concept of work-life integration is in part based on the simple fact that if most of your adult life is spent at work, how can you realize a better life without realizing better work? And given that your Desired Nature of Existence is such a critical variable in determining your point, you should look at how you exist today and specifically, how much you exist at work versus non-work.

Let's use my recent reality as the example. I worked at Harvard approximately twelve hours per day during the week and another few hours on the weekends. So, let's say my total work existence was sixty-six hours per week. By the way, a 2008 Harvard Business School survey of one thousand white-collar professionals determined that 94 percent of people work fifty hours or more per week and almost 50 percent work in excess of sixty-five hours per week. Ten years later, I have to imagine those numbers have gone way up, making me pretty much a slacker.

So, I got home from work at 6:30 p.m., I went to bed at 10:00 p.m. (exciting life, I know), and I was awake and not working around twenty-eight hours in total on Saturday and Sunday. My entire non-work, awake "life time" was 45.5 hours per week. I spent almost 50 percent more time in my work existence than I did in my life existence. Holy moly. Therefore, counselor, if I want to realize a better life, it's clear I must align my work with my point and my life.

Have I convinced you yet? And if I haven't, why don't you do your own math? Like right now.

The people you work with are the people you live with.

Your math or mine will always pretty much prove that we spend more time with people at work than we do with people at home, including our loved ones. That's kind of shocking, right? So, harkening back to Lesson #5: *There Are Only Two Tribes*, the question is whether some, all, or any of the people you work with are members of your Tribe. If not, imagine what that might be doing to your psyche and your quest to get to a better life. People need people (or cats) to evolve. And not just any people, but the right people. So, if you've surrounded your Self with the wrong people at work, your evolutionary capacity is effectively being thwarted. And given how hard personal evolution is, even with an acceptable level of rock-bottom motivation, we don't need that now, do we?

This Tribe-at-work question also reveals how little due diligence we tend to do when we interview for new jobs. Or rather, how our due diligence often focuses solely on the functional stuff (What will I do if I work here? How much will I make?) versus the feeling stuff (How does it feel to work here? What are people like here?) The people we work with and the cultures of the organizations we work for have a huge impact on our ability to be happy, to realize our full Selves, and to reach our point. A 2016 study by the Society of Human Resources Management on Employee Satisfaction decreed:

"Cultivate culture. Value-centric Millennials typically place high importance on openness, equality, community, and purpose (although, according to this research, all employees are looking for these types of aspects). Transparency and fairness generate trust. In addition, building an inclusive feel within the organization will help establish an emotional connection between the employee and the employer."[49]

An emotional connection with your employer. Imagine that. And imagine how focusing on feeling versus function might change your line of questioning and answering during the interview process. Assuming you're employed right now, why not go back in time to your first interview and contemplate the questions you'd ask then knowing what you know (and value) now? I'm guessing most of them would have to do with feeling and environmental stuff, right?

In my work advising students and managing the staff of the Harvard Innovation Labs, I always sought emotional connections in my exchanges. By that, I mean that since my point was to help every individual achieve his or her point, the conversations I had were usually about who and how they were, and how they wanted to be, versus what it was they were doing. I started most one-on-one meetings asking the other person how he or she felt. Okay, so some small percentage of them probably thought I was a freak, but the vast majority didn't. In fact, I sensed they felt relief realizing that we were going to have a conversation as people, not as functions. And over time our one-on-ones became more and more honest and emotionally grounded, which meant helpful to them and to me on our work-and-life-as-one journeys. And that is exactly what a work environment and any manager-employee relationship should yield. It's also what high-performing work environments are built on. Trust. And it was proven by Google.

In 2016 the *New York Times* published an article about Google's Project Aristotle, its rigorously researched effort to crack the code on what the key attributes of high-performing teams are. And it turns out the primary ingredient is trust: trust as measured by everyone on the team feeling like they have an equal voice, that their voice is worthy, and that their voice is trusted. The second attribute? Everyone on the team feels like the other team members have empathy for them—empathy, the not-so-distant cousin of trust. And third, the idea that in their participation on the team they are allowed to be who they are and not have to pretend to be somebody else—that they are trusted unconditionally.

When you work in an environment of trust, an environment that reflects and nurtures your true Self, you will soar. And when you don't, when you suffer work-life "dis-integration," you will stand still, or worse, head in the opposite direction.

The work-life integration dashboard.

A fully integrated work-and-life-as-one existence effectively presents a whole new set of success measures, a dashboard of sorts that informs whether you're getting closer to your point and whether the facets of your work and life are lining up just so. The old measures are, well, old. Things like job title, salary, size of office, and company prestige are replaced with very different metrics: Happiness. Growth. Alignment. Comfort.

Motivation. Instead of marking time, plodding our way to the end of the day, we focus on how we're feeling. We replace the largely functional and external metrics of success with qualitative metrics that reflect our inside.

(IM: What might the dials be on your work-life integration dashboard?)

The many dark sides of work-life dis-integration.

Work-life dis-integration, the lack of connectivity between what you do for a living and how you want to live, has a multitude of nasty side effects. The first, and most obvious, is the feeling of dissatisfaction as captured in that now ubiquitous expression, "I hate my job!" But dissatisfaction and hatred are just the veneer emotions that hide the real impact. When you hate your job, you create latent anger, which yields negative energy. And negative energy pushes positive energy away. Good things don't come to angry people. Ever. Good luck getting unstuck.

Job dissatisfaction and hatred also make Self-Love (Lesson #4) virtually impossible. Angry states of mind are the domain of Ego. If you hate your job, you probably don't love your Self. And instead of being able to focus on the wonder of you, you spend all your time wondering about how to find another job. Not good. The third big ugly consequence of having the wrong job or working for the wrong company is the *S* word: Stress. According to a 2016 Harvard School of Public Health Study, 59 percent of workers say their current job has an impact on their stress levels. The funny thing about stress is that, contrary to perception, it actually has very little to do with working too hard. It's the nature of the work that's the real issue. Simon Sinek, the TED Talks "Golden Circle" guy, said this about that:

"Working hard for something we don't care about is called stress: Working hard for something we love is called passion."[50]

Stress is fundamentally demotivating, destabilizing, and can be physically debilitating. While not perfectly proven, a slew of studies point to the likely fact that higher levels of stress contribute to a range of chronic health conditions and diseases. And let's ponder that word "disease" this way: dis-ease. So, the opportunity to achieve true work-life integration is not just about building a better life; it could be about saving your life. Think about that for a second.

Why is work-life integration so absurdly hard?

Now, my guess is that you may be saying to your Self (and to me) something like the following: "Okay, okay, I get the work-life integration thing, but making it happen just ain't that easy." I agree. But why would you stay in a job you hate? What is so damn difficult about finding a job that aligns with who we are and how we want to live? After all, as employees we are not indentured servants, we are not being held captive, and we are not required to stay, right? What's going on here? How is it possible that more people are willing to walk away from a dissatisfying marriage than a dissatisfying job? Well, in some cases job prospects really are slim, and making a move when you've got two little ones that need to be fed is pretty much impossible. Again, I get this. But I also get that many of us do have a choice, do have the latitude to make a change. So, for the lucky us, why do we stay put? Why are we doing work we hate?

The answer in part to all of the above lies with something we talked about in Chapter One: familiarity. It turns out a familiar job, even if dissatisfying, provides a comfort that the unfamiliar does not. So, we'll sacrifice our desire for more and better in exchange for less, but less with the comfort of the familiar.

Maslow again. (By the way, this is also the reason most people who read this book won't actually do anything that I have suggested. The familiar trumps doing the new. Don't be one of them, come on!)

But there's something else going on. Turns out people stay in crappy jobs because they don't know what kind of work they want *or* the work they want will pay them much less than what they "need" to make. The reason they don't know what kind of work they want is because they haven't done the work of defining their Selves. They haven't done their balance sheet. They don't know what their point is. They don't get their Passion, or Unique Capacities, or their Desired Nature of Existence. They either haven't read this book, or worse, they've avoided doing the exercises. And without those exercises done, without your attributes identified, how could you possibly know what kind of job, employer, or environment you want?

As for the money thing, it's real. We have to pay the bills, including that ridiculous one from the cable company. But that underscores that there are really two money numbers to consider: the money you think you need to make and the money you actually need to make. The difference between the two and your capacity to give up income and the stuff you buy with it is really a question of motivation and nailing what really matters to you. It turns out achieving work-life integration, achieving your point, and realizing a better life are all based on the same set of fundamental questions:

- How much do you want it (how desperate are you?)
- Are you willing to take on your fears?
- Are you okay with walking away from familiar things (including money)?

- Are you willing to give up comfort and cash to create the life you want?

- Are you willing to do the work to avoid the terrible fate of looking back at your life with regret?

Picture this Norman Rockwellian scene: My eldest brother Gary's retirement dinner at my sister Melissa's home a couple of years back. Twelve of us sitting around her mahogany dining room table, candles lit, wine glasses full. It's a celebration of his forty years working for National Geographic in their book production department. Forty years that resulted in a decent pension, for sure, but also forty years of work-life disintegration that resulted in him sharing this little ditty with my eldest son AJ and those around the table: "AJ, whatever you do, don't do what I did and sacrifice your life for your work."

(IM: What's holding you back from achieving your own work-life integration?)

Making work-life integration happen.

Okay, hopefully, I've got you appropriately agitated and ready to march toward an integrated work-life existence. If so, your next question is probably, "How exactly do I do this?" The flip answer is, do everything I tell you to do in this book and you'll make it happen. It's true, it's true, and let's quickly review:

Lesson #1: Evolve or Else. If you don't like what you do for a living, if it doesn't feel right, commit to changing the equation. Commit, commit, commit.

Lesson #2: The Point Is the Point. You can't leave the work you have without some sense of the kind of work-life you want to live. Define your point.

Lesson #3: You Need a Map to Realize Your Point. You've got to plan your way out of where you are in order to get to where you want to be. Sending out a bunch of résumés to a bunch of random organizations is not a plan. It's two steps away from playing craps at a casino, and dare I say, it almost always results in you losing. As declared, wishful thinking is not a map. Start contemplating and then start writing.

Lesson #4: Self-Love Is the Accelerant. If you don't love your Self, if Ego is controlling your actions and inactions, your ability to achieve work-life integration is effectively nil. The only way to get unstuck from your crappy job or career is to start loving your Self.

Lesson #5: There Are Only Two Tribes. And you can only find work that aligns with you and your Point if that workplace has plenty of your Tribe inside. Does it?

Lesson #6: Work and Life Are One. Do all of the above, and this will happen. I promise.

Lesson #7: It's All a Choice. While we haven't covered this rule yet, you get it, right? Doing the above is a choice. So, which choices are you going to make? See the final chapter for more explanation about this.

Some other hopefully helpful hints to achieve work-life integration.

Here are some other things you can do to increase your odds of improving the work part of the work-life integration equation.

Follow the leaders.

Assuming you want a job versus starting your own business, I bet you dollars to doughnuts that the kind of company that feels right to you is run by a person who leads the way you would want to be led. This is a dimension of the Tribe thing.

I truly believe that the ways of companies, their cultures, and their values are directly derivative of the way, culture, and values of their leaders. Find a progressive, open, caring leader, and you will find a progressive, open, caring company chock-full of your Tribespeople. So, instead of focusing your job search on companies, focus it on their leaders, and as we discussed, how it might feel to work there. Websites like Glassdoor can give you the inside scoop on which employers get it and which ones don't. And as you find these leaders and their companies, write down their names. Then start looking for people you know who know them. Proceed to the next hint.

Your work-life net worth will be a function of your network.

When looking for just the right work place or path, 99 percent of the opportunities will come from who you know and who knows you—which means get out there, please. Every day is a chance to build your network by restoring old connections and creating new ones.

The bigger your network, the greater the chances that someone in it will help you find just the right work environment, one that reflects who you are and how you want to be. The challenge, of course, with networking is that it's scary. People ask me all the time for my networking techniques. And my answer is three simple words: Courage, Content, and Curiosity. To be a great networker, you must first have the courage to put your hand out and say hello. Once again, fear is the great disabler of our desires. Get over it by considering what's at stake: your life.

The second C, Content, is about having something to say. One of the challenges of networking is that you have no idea who you are going to talk with and what they will want to talk about. And that feeds on your fears. The way to be a great networker is to be a great conversationalist, capable of chatting about pretty much anything to anybody. And that requires that you have knowledge, which requires that you consume a lot of content all the time. And I do mean all the time. My view on this one is that more is more and any content is good content, but you've got to diversify your sources. If Facebook and destination TV are your only content sources, umm, I don't want to talk to you. My content sources include *The New York Times, The Atlantic, The New Yorker*, the *Boston Globe* on weekends, *Bon Appetit, Architectural Digest, Art News, Vogue*—yes, *Vogue*—a slew of bedside table books, both fiction and nonfiction, and TV news when I am working out. It all contributes to my being able to parry about pretty much anything with pretty much anybody. If you find my list daunting, I have a dirty little secret: read *The Week* or *The Skim*. Both are composite weekly or daily digests of all the stuff you need to know to hold your own at the next gig.

And if you're not really that keen on the Content approach, at least adopt the third C, Curiosity. A large part of being a good networker involves being genuinely curious about the people you meet and good at asking them basic questions about the past, present, and future. The good news is that most people love to talk about themselves. You just need to prime their pump with your curiosity.

You don't know what you don't know.

Another aspect of the paralysis associated with being unable to go after work-life integration involves simply not knowing what is out there. You know where you are isn't working, but you have no idea what jobs, careers, and environments might fit you better. And as we've discussed, you may not have any idea what your Point and Passion(s) are. That's completely okay and totally normal. The key is exposing your Self to what's out there.

And there's a lot out there. In his *New York Times* opinion piece titled "Mis-Educating the Young," David Brooks wrote:

> "When I graduated from college there was a finite number of career ladders in front of me: teacher, lawyer, doctor, business. Now college graduates enter a world with four million footstools."[51]

You've got to start stepping on some footstools. You've got to both expose your Self to new paths while researching all the careers, industries, roles, and pathways that may or may not work for you. If you don't try to identify the possibilities, it's brutally hard and maybe even impossible to realize them.

Starting your own business may be the ultimate work-life integration.

For those who aren't keen on finding work-life integration by working for the man, or someone else, there is always the option of starting your own business. And depending on your Point, your Passion, your Unique Capacities, and the Desired Nature of Your Existence, this may, in fact, be the best path possible. In her compelling book *The Conscious Entrepreneur*, Laura Cannon talks about dissolving boundaries between work and life and realizing that "for your business to fully realize its potential, you need to fully realize your potential."[52] When people start businesses that align with their Point, they are already a long way toward meaningful work-life integration.

Create some milestones.

Remember Lesson #3: You Need a Map to Realize Your Point? Even if you aren't willing to do the map thing, how about some simple milestones or what we could call micro-points? What say you write down a handful of steps you want to take, time-based goals you want to accomplish that relate to your effort to achieve work-life integration. And then stick them on the refrigerator or on the wall of some frequently visited spot (the potty works). As silly as this sounds, these little pieces of paper (not the potty paper) are remarkably effective at holding us accountable.

Live beneath your means.

I can't imagine that you're liking this final hint. As I shared earlier, one of the big blockades to people quitting their disintegrated, dissatisfying jobs is that the job they want, the job or path that aligns with who they actually are, pays far less than what they need to make. And, they fear any amount of transition time between jobs because they simply don't have the savings to enable the bridge period. In both cases, they are financially stuck. They are effectively not-so-golden handcuffed. Both money issues lead to this simple but not-so-simple hint: Live beneath your means. Spend less than you could and save more than you would, and in doing so you create the latitude to follow your heart and integrate your life and work. Without financial breathing room, you and your life will be asphyxiated.

The challenge, of course, is that spending less really means sacrificing more. And who the hell wants to sacrifice? Funnily or not so funnily enough, we're back to the question of motivation and the lovely construct called "acceptable rock bottom." If you are desperate to change your lot in life and get to a better life, sacrifice isn't so big a deal. If you're not quite to the bottom, giving up what you have to get what you want becomes a Sisyphean, read impossible, task.

Consider a pivot instead of a punt.

There's a baby-step option, too. Instead of walking away from your current job and employer in order to realize your work and life as one, what about looking for another environment and gig within your current company? Is it possible that your work-life dis-integration issue is less a function of the overall environment and more the issues around your specific job, department, and maybe even boss? If so, you could, and maybe even should, consider pivoting where you are versus punting and looking for a brand spanking new line of work.

Doing is not living.

Enough hints, enough tasks. Let's cut to the chase. Work-life integration is not about some ideal combination of doing things at work and home; it's about doing only one thing: being. It's about each of us grasping that just being is the essential form of a fully realized life, a life that has achieved its point, a life that has the richest meaning. Being who we are, being how we want to be, and being our Passions and Unique Capacities regardless of work or life context. That is the opportunity and the challenge. Sure, it's hard, but so is looking back and wishing we'd done it all differently.

Three Things You Should Do Now

1. Crank up the networking. Set a goal of meeting and connecting with three new people a week. I don't care who they are or what they do. Just apply the three C's and start saying hello.

2. Do the ten-person Traits of Tribespeople exercise from Chapter 5 again, but this time only consider the ten people at work whom you spend the most time with. It might cause minor heart palpitations, but that's okay; you can do something about it.

3. Try living beneath your means. Start saving money and creating work-life as one latitude by identifying three ongoing expenses you could kill or cut in half. Kate and I spend $102 per month on a storage unit full of stuff we will never use. Actually, we can't remember what's in it. It's going.

it's all a choice

So, here we are, at the end, which could in short order become your new beginning. And the final, most fundamental question is *What now?* Sure, I want you to apply the seven lessons, I want you to dig deep and find your source of motivation, and I want you to embrace the concepts of Self-Love, the Tribe, the map, and all the other stuff. But before you really start working on all that, I would like you to take a step back, look at your entire life to this point, and ask your Self this very simple question:

How did all this happen, and how in the name of the Talking Heads did I get here?

Well, I have some good or bad news depending on your current disposition. Where you are didn't happen to you. You made it happen.

More often than not, our current reality is a function not of "externalities" but of the decisions and non-decisions we have made along the way. And that deliciously sets up the final lesson, the mother of all lessons, Lesson #7: *It's All a Choice. Our ability to innovate our life, to realize our point, is largely based on our choices.* Period, end of paragraph, and almost end of book. But let me dig into this a little more. Because this is really important.

We are what we choose.

Every action we take is a choice, a decision to do or not to do something, or to do it in a certain way. Every day is a blank piece of paper that we fill in, sometimes with intention, more often without. I get up at 4:35 a.m. every day. A choice. A crazy one, but a choice nonetheless. I worked for three plus years at Harvard. A choice. Whether it's crazy or not will be revealed in a soon-to-be-published tell-all book. I yearn to paint and draw but do not. A choice. I call my ailing mother every few days. A choice, even though I know I should call her every day. My retirement savings are not where I want them to be. A choice. It's all a choice. Your life when you look back will either be full of joy and the good choices you made or full of regret and the choices you wish you had made. Remember the *Top Five Regrets of the Dying* book I mentioned in the Intro? All of the regrets are about people not making the right choices, not choosing to build intimate relationships, and not choosing to follow their hearts, to go after their points.

You know that expression "Life is too short"? Well, this cutting-edge philosopher and statesman from around AD 20 named Lucius Seneca the Younger penned a compelling treatise suggesting it wasn't really an issue of length but rather of the choices we make along the way that determines a sufficient and worthy life. He opined:

> "It is not that we have a short space of time, but that we waste much of it. Life is long enough, and it has been given in sufficiently generous measure to allow the accomplishment of the very greatest things if the whole of it is well invested."[53]

If it is well invested. Catch that? Well-invested equals making good choices. So, that's the task moving forward for you, for me, for everyone who is seeking a better life. Not simply to try to apply *This Is It* lessons, but to make all the right choices, the right investments that help you get to where you want to get to, your point. Making the right choices pretty much requires clarity regarding where you are trying to go. And guts. More on that shortly.

By the way, as a way of underscoring how much harder it is to do this stuff than to declare it, poor Seneca made the bad choice of becoming Emperor Nero's advisor, which ultimately resulted in the two-screws-loose Nero demanding that Seneca commit suicide as part of a purge. Which he did. Another choice.

Be the writer, not the written.

Way back when in Chapter One, I introduced the idea of *Your Life,* the movie, and tried to help you see that if you don't evolve, if you don't go after your point, the final movie about your life will probably pretty much suck. The underlying issue here is whether you are operating as the screenwriter or the cameraman. Are you allowing circumstance and random choices to define your plot and the resulting consequences, or are you taking the pen by the horns and making the right choices that will result in a great story being crafted and lived? And you know you only have one shot at your story, a story that necessarily includes your work and your life outside of work (Lesson #6). The clock is ticking, my friend. There are only so many hours you can keep the actors on the stage. The audience has a short attention span.

Whatever your reason, you've got to be the writer and you've got to make the right choices, and fast. And remember those words of Carl Jung, the shrink of all shrinks, "I am not what happened to me; I am what I choose to become."[54] Choose to write your life.

And if you don't find that sufficiently motivating, do the following:

Consider the consequences.

What if we could see the downstream impact of all our choices? What if we had an Opportunity Cost calculator app on our phone? What if there was a flashing red LED display in our kitchen that was a countdown of how many hours we have left on earth? Wouldn't it change our approach to choice? Wouldn't we think twice about the investments we were or were not making, about how we were frittering away our precious life, or perhaps avoiding taking the risks to get what we really want? The consequences are huge, and yet we have a hard time seeing them. Until the end. And then it's all brutally clear. I'm hesitant to do this, but I'm going to share another Steve Jobs quote that sadly but all too effectively captures my point:

> "Remembering that I'll be dead soon is the most important tool I've ever encountered to help me make the big choices in life. Because almost everything—all external expectations, all pride, all fear of embarrass-ment or failure—these things just fall away in the face of death, leaving only what is truly important."[55]

Too many of us need death to value life, need calamity to force clarity, need desperation (sound familiar?) to enable risk-taking and stepping forward to what we want. You've been there; I know you have. A friend or family member passes away. The day you hear about it, you breathe the air differently. You value things you didn't value the day before. You call a friend you haven't spoken to in ages. You tell your parents you love them. Loss motivates an appreciation of living and a desire to live it with more gusto, to take more risk. And to make better choices, choices that align with our point and our effort to realize a better life. But then, after a while, we forget and go back to the way we were. Stuck and fearful.

It's quite remarkable, really. For a moment we get it, perhaps even for a few days. And then the clarity fades, the motivation to live our lives differently dissipates, and we fall back to making bad choices or no choices at all. Until the next loss, or perhaps until we wake up on our deathbed surrounded by pillows of regret. It does not have to be this way, which makes that the ultimate choice.

Why we are so bad at making good choices.

How people make decisions may be one of the most-researched topics in the world, in part because we are nothing but our decisions, right? Instead of delving into such heady issues as the irrationality of decision-making and cognitive bias, I'm going to give you a science-free perspective on what I think is really going on in terms of our poor ability to make good choices. I'm pretty sure it's just as valid, but you can be the judge.

Remember Lesson #2: The Point Is the Point? Well, one of the big reasons we struggle to make good choices is because we actually don't have a point, which really means we don't know what good is. Alison, the fictional friend who was trying to lose weight in Chapter Two (and probably still is), could not effectively decide whether her diet choices were right without some definition of what her weight loss/get healthy goal was. Without a clear point, choosing French fries smothered in cheese and gravy might sound just fine.

Fundamentally, you simply cannot assess the value of a choice and its short-term consequences without being able to hold it up to the collective future consequence, your desired point. Wise old Seneca the Younger also had this to say about that:

> "If one does not know to which port one is sailing, no wind is favorable."[56]

Absent a point, or port, most choices are not the best choice.

Alongside the need for a point is the ever-present influence of Maslow's Hierarchy of Need. By now you should readily accept that our very basic need state is the initial filter through which we put all decisions and choices. The foundational needs are all about comfort, control, and protection, which pretty much boil down to that debilitating thing called fear. Our primal, Ego-centric, Shadow Child selves are relentlessly fixated on having enough food, water, sex, and shelter and on making sure the bad people don't get us. Imagine the quality of our decision-making and our choices when we come from a place of fear.

(IM: Think about the last time you made a choice out of fear. Was it a good choice?)

Even if fear is in the back seat, the majority of our decisions and choices are made emotionally. Ponder for a second how you decided what college to attend, what apartment to rent, what job to take. Hell, even who you married. Did you build spreadsheets specifying the pros and cons on any of those decisions? Did you undertake rigorous research to identify the alternatives and weigh them against your established and prioritized selection criteria? Of course, you didn't. I didn't. Nobody does. Our choices are made on the basis of how we feel, less what we think. And while following our emotions feels good, it doesn't always end well or help us achieve our point.

While bad choices are the accidental spawn of missing points, primal fears, and the incessant presence of emotion, there's a fourth root cause. I call it nascent greed. We often make bad choices because we want what we want when we want it. We are junkies for immediate gratification, and we have a remarkable capacity to block out the downstream consequences so we can wallow in what feels good now. This applies to everything from deciding on a second helping of ice cream to having an affair. The mind's ability to suppress the negative impact of our decisions is quite remarkable. That's why 60 percent of Americans are obese and why, according to a slightly weird website DivorceStatistics.com, almost one in five marriages crater because someone chose to have an affair.

The fifth and final cause of our crappy decision-making is our lack of Self-Love. If we don't love our Selves, then we are subconsciously always seeking the love and validation of others. And when we seek that, we cannot possibly be clear-headed about the choices we want or need to make. In fact, the more we need acceptance from others, the more likely our choices are about them and not about us. I'm reminded of a conversation I had with my three now-grown children about why so many teenagers and college kids get black-out drunk. I asked them why kids choose to get so wasted. And the answer was some combination of seeking acceptance and getting over their shyness, a.k.a. a lack of Self-Love and fear.

Love & courage: the path to better choices.

Whatever the causal factors, at the end of the day your ability to make better choices, your ability to realize your point and all the attributes of a better life, is fundamentally tied to Self-Love and one specific behavior, which turns out to be a choice, too. And that behavior is your ability to choose courage over fear as the guiding light of your life. Making choices from a position of courage gives you clarity, the capacity to take risk, the willingness to listen to your heart, and more. Making choices from a position of fear results in the opposite.

Martha Beck, the author of *Finding Your Own North Star* agrees:

> "When fear makes your choices for you, no security measures on earth will keep the things you dread from

finding you. But if you can avoid avoidance—if you can choose to embrace experiences out of passion, enthusiasm, and a readiness to feel whatever arises—then nothing, nothing in all this dangerous world, can keep you from being safe."[57]

I used to think that courage was innate. That you either had it or you didn't. I now believe that courage and fear are in all of us; that what separates the seemingly brave ones from the not so brave is that the brave ones simply choose courage over fear more often. I have come to see that my life is made up of many "moments of choice" and that in the moments that conjure up fear, picking courage is always an option. You can pick courage to jump off a diving board. You can pick courage to tell your boss you want a raise. You can pick courage to work on your point. You can pick courage to begin to get unstuck. In fact, you must.

In my daily existence, I am fully aware of the choice moments that I experience where the option of courage over fear is, well, an option. I am also aware that ten years ago I pretty much always chose fear in those moments. I chose fear when I entered a room of strangers; I chose fear when I went into a store because, perhaps ironically, I was going to have to make choices; I chose fear when I thought about telling my now ex-wife the truth about how I felt about pretty much everything.

Ten years later, I choose courage a lot more, but not always. When I have to present to a large group of people, I often feel a little fear but choose courage. I kind of have to! When I want to talk to my wife Kate about something she has done that bothers me, I feel fear but choose courage—not always, but that's okay. It's okay that you don't always choose courage. What really matters is that we are aware of these moments, aware of our choices, and over time get better at picking courage over fear as their foundation.

Each lesson is a choice.

It's all a choice. And that includes this book's seven lessons. The only thing that separates you from where you want to be, your point, is your decision to do something, your choice.

So, here are some summary choices for you to make. Please repeat after me.

I choose to evolve. I now find the prospect of standing still for the rest of my life totally unacceptable. I want more meaning than what I have now; I am at or close to rock bottom.

I choose to determine my point. I know I don't want to do the work; in fact, I'm a little scared about what it might reveal, but I am going to pick courage and figure out the Why of me and how I want to be.

I choose to make a map to help me realize my point. Again, I don't want to do the work, but I realize that without a solid, plotted map, I will probably go around in circles. And that is downright silly.

I choose to love my Self. I understand that it is not a flicking of a switch, and that it will be a difficult and sometimes painful journey to get to this place. But I am ready. And I'm kinda cute.

I choose to find my Tribe. I will no longer surround my Self with people who dishonor me or who simply don't understand the importance of the journey I am on. If my birth family members are not members of my Tribe, I accept that and I love them, but I will not allow them to weigh me down.

I choose to work toward work-life integration. I will do everything I can to align what I do with who I am and how I want to be.

I choose to make better choices, choices grounded in courage, choices that honor me, respect me, and help me realize my point and the kind of life I seek.

And finally, I already know all this stuff. **I choose** to apply this knowledge to my life, for the rest of my life, in order to realize a better life.

You can do this.

This is not rocket science. Sure, filling out your Balance Sheet can be challenging, and some of the other introspective exercises may be gut-wrenching and befuddling, but you're not being tasked with curing cancer. You're being tasked with curing your life. And there's good news in that: *You can do this.* You just need to find your motivation, choose to go forward, and start going. It will take time and real effort. It will take courage and resilience. And most importantly, it will take other people. Your Tribe. So, find more of them. You've already found me.

Three Things You Can Do Now

1. Practice choosing courage. Look for courage versus fear moments in the week ahead. Contemplate how the moments feel, and work toward picking courage in a moment that you would normally pick fear. Selecting strange menu items is always a good primer.

2. Shift your time horizon. As you contemplate making different and better choices, stop focusing on tomorrow and start looking toward the longer term. That's where your point lies.

3. Reread this book every year. As inspired as you might be right now, it will be hard to maintain that motivation. You'll lose steam, things will come up, you might even find temporary cures. My hope is that skimming this book every year (maybe make it a birthday gift to yourself?) might provide the necessary kick in the pants to keep you innovating, keep you on the path to your point, to a more satisfying life.

And for the final, book-ending, motivational quote from Dr. Jung:

> "Every human life contains a potential; if that potential is not fulfilled, then that life is wasted . . ."[58]

What he said.

May your choices be good ones. May your innovations be bold.

And may your life be amazing. Because this is it.

Chris

one last thing
you can do now

As you now know, the point of my life, of my being on this planet, is to help people. The point of this book is to help people. And hopefully it helped you. If it did, I would love it if you would spread the word by talking it up with your friends (in your Tribe of course), giving it a thumbs up review on GoodReads.com and bookseller sites, and maybe even signing up at chriscolbert.com to get my monthly Blueberry, a short and sweet bit of commentary on how we can make more out of the only lives we will be given. Think of it as a friendly and consistent booster shot.

You can also find more boosters here:

Facebook: https://www.facebook.com/chris.colbert.1690
Twitter: https://twitter.com/chriscolbertX
LinkedIn: https://www.linkedin.com/in/colbertprofile/
Medium: https://medium.com/@chriscolbert

Thanks for your help.

Chris

to my partners in publishing:

Y ou would not be reading this without the wise guidance, occasional cajoling, and unwavering support provided by several partners: Ally Machate, the CEO of The Writer's Ally who held my hand from start to finish; Sherrie Clark, the CEO of Storehouse Media Group who turned my manuscript into a compelling little book available to the world; Brett William, my brilliant friend and creative mind who pushed me on the title and delivered a cover like no other; and to a number of friends who read the rough drafts and gave me incredibly helpful feedback.

I've learned a lot about the journey of making a book, and the biggest learn is that you can't do it alone.

endnotes and bibliography

1 Jobs, Steve. 2005 commencement address, Stanford University.
https://news.stanford.edu/2005/06/14/jobs-061505

2 Ryan, Patrick. "How 'Collateral Beauty' helped Will Smith say goodbye to his father." *USA Today*, December 13, 2016.
https://www.usatoday.com/story/life/movies/2016/12/13/collateral-beauty-will-smith-jacob-latimore/95109620/

3 Pressfield, Steven. *The War of Art*. Black Irish Entertainment, 2012.

4 Ibid.

5 Chopra, Deepak. *The Seven Spiritual Laws of Success*. Amber-Allen Publishing, 2011.

6 Unknown. https://www.snopes.com/news/2017/02/13/gop-misattributed-inspirational-lincoln-quote/

7 Jung, Carl. *Memories, Dreams, Reflections*. Pantheon Books, 1963.

8 Thompson, Derek. "The Four Letter Code to Selling Just About Anything." *The Atlantic,* January/February, 2017.
https://www.theatlantic.com/magazine/archive/2017/01/what-makes-things-cool/508772

9 Kabat-Zimm, Jon. *Wherever You Go, There You Are*. Hyperion Books, 1994.

10 Lang, Amanda. *The Power of Why*. Collins, 2012.

11 Harari, Yoval Noah. *21 Lessons for the 21st Century*. Spiegel & Grau, 2018.

12 J.K. Rowling, 2008 commencement address, Harvard University.
https://news.harvard.edu/gazette/story/2008/06/text-of-j-k-rowling-speech/

13 Covey, Stephen. *7 Habits of Highly Effective People*. Free Press, 2004.

14 Iarovici, Doris. "The Antidepressant Generation." *The New York Times*, April 17, 2014. https://well.blogs.nytimes.com/2014/04/17/the-antidepressant-generation

15 George, Bill. *True North*. John Wiley & Sons, 2015.

16 Collins, Jim and Porras, Jerry. *Built to Last*. HarperBusiness, 1994.

17 Unknown

18 Sinek, Simon. *Start with Why*. Penguin Group, 2009.

19 Chopra, Deepak. *The Seven Spiritual Laws of Success*. Amber-Allen Publishing, 2011.

20 McNamara, Garrett. *Hound of the Sea*. HarperCollins Publishers, 2016.

21 Davis, Jr., Sammy.

22 Rumelt, Richard. *Good Strategy Bad Strategy*. Currency, 2011.

23 Petridis, Alexis. "Shakira." *The Guardian*, October 15, 2009. https://www.theguardian.com/music/2009/oct/15/shakira-interview

24 Bon Jovi, Jon. 2015 commencement address, Rutgers University-Camden. http://time.com/collection-post/3892791/bon-jovi-graduation-speech-rutgers-camden/

25 Ray, Oakley. https://www.ncbi.nlm.nih.gov/pubmed/15677394

26 Voltaire

27 Lyon, George Ella. *Holding on to Zoe*. Macmillan, 2012.

28 Ball, Lucille.

29 Tolle, Eckhart. *The Power of Now*. Namaste Publishing, 2004.

30 Paul, Margaret. "Fear of Intimacy." *Thrive Global*, November 15, 2017. https://thriveglobal.com/stories/fear-of-intimacy

31 Fromm, Erich. *The Art of Loving*. Harper and Row, 1956.

32 Harris, Russ. *The Happiness Trap*. Trumpeter Books, 2007.

33 O'Sullivan, Michael. "Noah Baumbach, (almost) all grown up." *The Washington Post*, April 2, 2015.
https://www.washingtonpost.com/entertainment/noah-baumbach-almost-all-grown-up/2015/04/02/69ec728a-d6f9-11e4-8103-fa84725dbf9d_story.html?utm_term=.259f0b4000f3

34 Bryan, Mark, with Julia Cameron and Catherine Allen. *The Artist's Way at Work*. Jeremy P Tarcher/Putnam, 1992.

35 Ibid

36 Palmer, Parker. *A Hidden Wholeness*. Jossey-Bass, 2004.

37 Masson, Jeffrey. *Dogs Never Lie About Love*. Crown, 1997.

38 Taylor, Madisyn. "United in Thought and Action." Reprinted from DailyOM – Inspirational thoughts for a happy, healthy and fulfilling day.
https://www.dailyom.com/cgi-bin/display/articledisplay.cgi?aid=60286&aff

39 Gorski, Terence T. *Getting Love Right*. Fireside, 1993.

40 Aletta, Elvira. Multiple texts on https://psychcentral.com/blog/what-makes-a-family-functional-vs-dysfunctional/ and https://www.explorewhatsnext.com/

41 Palmer, Parker. *A Hidden Wholeness*. Jossey-Bass, 2004.

42 Ibid

43 Moyer, Bill. "What they told the class of '88. On bread and community." *The Christian Science Monitor*, July 27, 1988.
https://www.csmonitor.com/1988/0727/ubread.html

44 Vanderkam, Laura. *I Know How She Does It*. Portfolio, 2015.

45 Jobs, Steve. 2005 commencement address, Stanford University.
https://news.stanford.edu/2005/06/14/jobs-061505

46 Douglas, Dean. "Why Work-Life Integration Trumps Work-Life Balance." *Fast Company*, May 7, 2014.
https://www.fastcompany.com/3030120/why-work-life-integration-trumps-work-life-balance

[47] Burnett, Bill. *Designing Your Life.* Alfred A. Knopf, 2016.

[48] Cope, Stephen. *The Great Work of Your Life.* Bantam Books, 2012.

[49] Society for Human Resource Management. "2016 Employee Job Satisfaction and Engagement: Revitalizing a Changing Workforce." https://www.shrm.org/hr-today/trends-and-forecasting/research-and-surveys/Pages/Job-Satisfaction-and-Engagement-Report-Revitalizing-Changing-Workforce.aspx

[50] Sinek, Simon. *Start with Why.* Penguin Group, 2009.

[51] Brooks, David. "Mis-Educating the Young." *The New York Times,* June 23, 2017. https://www.nytimes.com/2017/06/23/opinion/mis-educating-the-young.html

[52] Cannon, Laura. *The Conscious Entrepreneur.* One Tribe Press, 2015.

[53] Seneca the Younger, Lucius. A Letter to Paulinus. https://fs.blog/2017/03/seneca-on-the-shortness-of-time/

[54] Jung, Carl. *Memories, Dreams, Reflections.* Pantheon Books, 1963.

[55] Jobs, Steve. 2005 commencement address, Stanford University. https://news.stanford.edu/2005/06/14/jobs-061505.

[56] Seneca the Younger, Lucius. *Letters from a Stoic.*

[57] Beck, Martha. *Finding Your Own North Star.* Three Rivers Press, 2001.

[58] Jung, Carl. *Memories, Dreams, Reflections.* Pantheon Books, 1963.

about the author

chris colbert

As the son of a Naval officer, Chris grew up living around the world, which caused him to wonder about the world. That led him to innovation. His father was a four-star admiral. That led him to leadership. Together, they have resulted in what some say is his unique ability to help organizations and individuals realize their unrealized potential by challenging convention, embracing the truth, and creating foundations for functional and behavioral growth.

From the early 1990s to 2005, he helped start and run several companies focused on innovation and technology, including Database Marketing Corporation, BeNow (sold to Equifax), and

Holland-Mark, a full-service agency and innovation-consulting firm. From 2007 to 2012, as CEO of Holland-Mark, he worked with a range of startups and enterprise scale businesses on growth and turnaround strategies by leveraging innovation best practices and achieving organizational alignment.

In 2012, he became Chairman Emeritus of Holland-Mark and took a position as SVP, Strategy at Scholastic Corporation in New York to help turn around its crown jewel Book Club division. After helping lead a revamp of the business and its return to positive growth, he left in early 2014, to explore the world of higher education and technology innovations that might help improve its price/value equation while helping their students transition to the real world. That led him to the Harvard Innovation Labs, where he served as managing director until May, 2019. He then left Harvard to co-found one eighty, a global innovation consultancy focused on helping companies and countries better compete by creating cultures of innovation.

In addition to his role running one eighty, Chris is an author of several books and speaks around the world on a range of topics covering innovation, technology, and humanity. He received a BA from Connecticut College, an International MBA from Duke's Fuqua School of Business, and sits on several boards.

His board work includes Grand Circle Corporation, the Leadership Council of the MGH Cancer Center, The Rose Kennedy Greenway Leadership Council, the MassArt Corporate Advisory Council, the Greater Boston Food Bank, Pillar Ventures, and Now + There, a nonprofit public art organization.

Chris can be reached at chris@chriscolbert.com and through www.chriscolbert.com.

9 781943 106479